THIS BOOK BELONGS TO ...

....

100% UNOFFICIAL

First published in Great Britain 2024 by 100% Unofficial,
a part of Farshore

An imprint of HarperCollinsPublishers
1 London Bridge Street, London SE1 9GF
www.farshore.co.uk

HarperCollinsPublishers
Macken House, 39/40 Mayor Street Upper,
Dublin 1 D01 C9W8 Ireland

Written by Kevin Pettman
Design by Cloud King Creative
Illustrations by Matt Burgess

This book is an original creation by Farshore
© 2024 Farshore

ISBN 978 0 00 861560 4
Printed and bound in Malaysia
1

ONLINE SAFETY FOR YOUNGER FANS

Spending time online is great fun! Here are a few simple rules to help younger
fans stay safe and keep the internet a great place to spend time.
• Never give out your real name – don't use it as your username.
• Never give out any of your personal details.
• Never tell anybody which school you go to or how old you are.
• Never tell anybody your password, except a parent or guardian.
• Be aware that you must be 13 or over to create an account on many sites.
Always check the site policy and ask a parent or guardian for permission before registering.
• Always tell a parent or guardian if something is worrying you.
Stay safe online. Any website addresses listed in this book are correct at the
time of going to print. However, Farshore is not responsible for content hosted by
third parties. Please be aware that online content can be subject to change and
websites can contain content that is unsuitable for children. We advise that
all children are supervised when using the internet.

FSC
www.fsc.org

MIX
Paper | Supporting
responsible forestry
FSC™ C007454

This book contains FSC™ certified paper and other controlled
sources to ensure responsible forest management.

For more information visit: www.harpercollins.co.uk/green

ROBLOX
100 TOP GAMES

CONTENTS

GREATEST GAMES!

Welcome to the Roblox universe! It's time for a fun-packed journey as you explore the greatest games and enjoy stacks of special on-screen adventures. Roblox has thousands of experiences to join in with, from town and city fun and tycoon domination, to obstacle, role-play, first-person shooters and many more. It's the best place for the ultimate gaming thrill!

How do you choose which games to play, though? Luckily, Roblox Top 100 Games is here to reveal a selection of the very best. This awesome guide features 100 of the greatest games, sorted into categories and numbered 1-100. How many have you played – and how many will you be inspired to try out?

Load up your device and get gaming!

WOW!
Around 58 million people play on Roblox every day!

TOWN AND CITY

Roblox games are grouped into genres and one of the most popular is town and city. These games are often set in an urban location and feature a fun mix of action, role-playing and collecting items and abilities to boost your game powers.

Check out the top town and city games!

TINY TOWN TYCOON

TINY TOWN TYCOON

DINOSAUR CITY SIM

AWARD WINNER
Welcome to Bloxburg, a hugely popular town and city game, won a Roblox Innovation Award in 2022. Unlike most of the big games, Bloxburg is not free to play.

ROCITIZENS

ROCITIZENS

MEEPCITY

POLIC

1 BROOKHAVEN

CREATED BY: **WOLFPAQ** YEAR: **2020**

With tens of billions of visits, Brookhaven is one of the leading Roblox attractions and adored by gamers! Fans of role-playing pack out this urban place and enjoy leading a fun digital life as they work, set up home, drive around and customise their avatars.

TOP TIP
Use your 10 item slots to equip tools such as a smartphone, binoculars, cash and food.

Choosing where to live is easy and free, with no need to spend Robux (Roblox's in-game currency). From modern, flashy pads with barbecues in the garden, to cool apartments by the airport, you can just claim a vacant place. Use the house security cams to watch your property … and don't forget to lock up when you leave!

You'll soon want to grab a car to move quickly around town. Tap the vehicle icon to choose from an exciting range of machines, including motorbikes, sports cars, buses and even tanks! Hit your max speed and take a trip to learn what's going on in the busy Brookhaven streets.

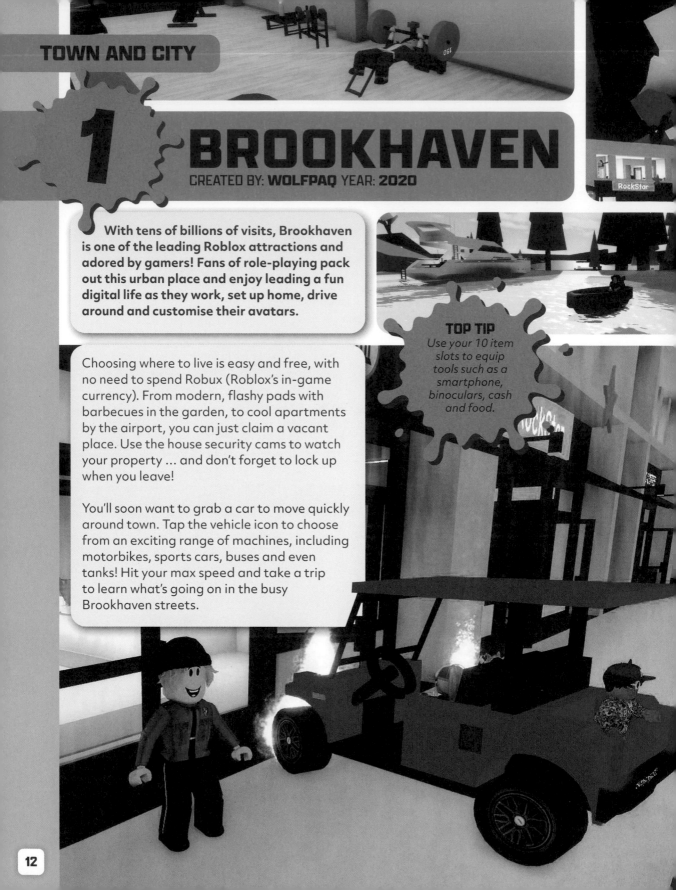

What job will you take? Perhaps working in a bank, a shop or on a plane will be fun? Don't worry if you want to relax again, because there's the option to take a work break or even quit your job. It's like you're always the boss in Brookhaven!

This town and city giant can have as many as 18 other gamers playing in the same session as you – and more than 500,000 Roblox fans are often on Brookhaven at the same time! If you have Robux to spend, the 2022 Disaster Pass takes the action to a new level as aliens, zombies and bugs can be unleashed. This town then becomes a total escape from reality!

2 LIVETOPIA

CREATED BY: **CENTURY MAKERS** YEAR: **2021**

There are often crossover town and city and role-playing games. Livetopia has lots of good stuff from both genres and it reached an impressive three billion visits within two years. The city of Topia is your playground, where you choose roles, houses, cars, friends, pets and loads more fun stuff.

Creators Century Makers are always updating Livetopia. In 2023 a cool new cinema, mall, hairdressers and cosmetic shops were included. One thing not quite so enjoyable was also created – a trip to the Topia dentist. Arrgghh!

Don't miss the many special appearances and seasonal twists in Livetopia. Halloween parks, obstacle courses and summer cruises have all appeared. Mariah Carey even performed an exclusive Christmas concert in this awesome digital world!

SMART MOVE
The easiest way to navigate Topia is with the map. Open the app, tap your destination and then follow the on-screen arrows to get there in no time!

3 WORK AT A PIZZA PLACE

CREATED BY: **DUED1** YEAR: **2008**

Created back in 2008 and clocking four billion visits by the end of 2022, Work at a Pizza Place is Roblox royalty! The idea is simple: choose to be a cashier, cook, delivery driver, pizza boxer, supplier or manager and collect coins to have a fun time in this mozzarella-mad world!

Luckily, it's not all about making and munching pizzas! With your earnings you can upgrade your house, adding great new features and furniture. Don't stay on your break too long, though, as you must pick up your pay cheque and keep the others you work with happy. Good teamwork is vital.

Becoming the pizza manager is the best prize! Move quickly to sit in the boss's chair as soon as it becomes free. Or, purchase the manager teleport pass to instantly occupy it when it's available. Be a nice boss or the workers may vote to remove you!

4 EMERGENCY RESPONSE: LIBERTY COUNTY

CREATED BY: **POLICE ROLE-PLAY COMMUNITY** YEAR: **2018**

Not all town and city games are as relaxed as Brookhaven. Emergency Response: Liberty County keeps players on constant alert as you take on exciting role-play quests in an epic battle for the good of River City or Springfield Town ... or for the bad if you become a criminal! That's right – you can choose to be bad!

Start by selecting your role. Choose from civilian, sheriff, firefighter, police officer or transport worker. Most new players begin as a regular civilian to help work out the functions and basic gameplay options. Civilians can easily become criminals, by committing a robbery or challenging the cops!

Doing bad things automatically puts you on the wanted system. Your wanted level status is shown by stars – the more stars you have, the more the police will try to throw you in jail. The life of a criminal is very risky in Emergency Response: Liberty County!

If you choose to be in the emergency services, listen for emergency calls. These are made by civilians or by the game itself. If you get a call, it's your duty to respond and deal with the incident, whether it's a robbery, a fire or any emergency. Use radio chat and your mobile data terminal (MDT) to view all the urgent details.

Responding well to emergencies gives the police, firefighters and transport workers the chance to boost their ranks. As a cop or sheriff, raising your status from cadet to sergeant or beyond gives you greater XP and even unlocks better and faster vehicles and weapons. Cool!

TOP TIP
Breaking into the bank using the lock pick gives criminals a very helpful 60-second advantage over the police!

5 GREENVILLE

CREATED BY: GREENVILLE, WISCONSIN YEAR: 2017

Town and city Roblox games have everything you'd expect to find in busy urban places, and in Greenville that means cars! So if you're motor-mad, this is the place to get your driving buzz. It's all about collecting cars, customising, getting cash and having fun behind the wheel.

FAST MOVES
Be quick to snap up an exclusive limited time car. These wicked wheels make you look awesome on the streets!

Your virtual garage is where your cool cars are stored. Sleek and stylish rides cost more and if you want to add fresh paintwork and top-level tyres, it all takes money. Luckily, there are a few ways to make cash in Greenville. Just driving around rewards your bank balance, but if you're speeding, you won't get as much!

As well as cars, Greenville gives you the chance to work at a job and build a house. There are around 50 jobs, from firefighter to burger maker, that earn a vital paycheck. Entering the car dealership with plenty of notes in your wallet is a cool feeling!

BURGERHAUS

6 MEEPCITY

CREATED BY: **ALEXNEWTRON** YEAR: **2016**

Looking for a relaxing town and city challenge? Jump into MeepCity to start your quest to play minigames, collect coins, set up a home and customise your awesome avatar! Plus, you do all this alongside your trusted pet, known as a Meep.

When you have coins, run to the pet shop and adopt a cute Meep! You can even name it by splashing out a further 150 coins. Don't forget to fish as well, because selling your catches at the pet shop is a great way to raise funds.

The kart racing game is also a fun part of MeepCity. It's like a mini go-kart track, with boosts to pick up and bananas to avoid on the course. You'll collect coins for how well you race, with 150 for the winner. Find it through the kart racing tunnel, inside the Toybox.

BUSY CITY
There can be as many as 200 players in a MeepCity game!

7 ROBLOX HIGH SCHOOL 2

CREATED BY: **CINDER STUDIO** YEAR: **2018**

The follow-up to the huge original Roblox High School, RHS 2 takes gamers to a world where education and fun role-play mix together in the city of Starcadia Bay. When you attend classes you earn credits and XP, which can then be used to buy a range of items around town. So, it really pays to go to school!

Open your brand new iCinder portable device to connect with the community. You can message friends, join a school club and check out your daily schedule. When you have a class to go to, a notification appears on the top of your screen.

A major update has added the city of Libra Rosa. When players reach level 25 in the game, Libra Rosa can be accessed and used as a clever trading hub, where credits and items can be exchanged with other players. This is a great way to earn more credits to spend!

DOUBLE DELIGHT
If you have Robux to spend, the double wages perk soon swells your bank balance.

8 ROCITIZENS

CREATED BY: **FIREBRAND1** YEAR: **2013**

RoCitizens gets great updates all the time, keeping it as fresh and fun as when it first launched in 2013! It's a town and city game with lots of role-playing mixed in. Your avatar explores RoCity, choosing work and building a brilliant life. Good luck!

Keep playing to pick up daily bonuses, ranging from $100 to $3,000. Getting a job is very important too. Make a note of the hourly rate, with hospital nurses earning $20 for looking after patients and bus drivers getting $25.

Getting a car is another priority. It will help you explore the neighbourhood, see the sights and make the most of life in RoCity. Use the helpful 3D map in the corner of the screen to navigate quickly and whenever Henry offers tips, listen to him carefully!

9 ROTUBE LIFE!

CREATED BY: **PLAY! STUDIOS** YEAR: **2022**

In this adventure you live the life of a top gamer, making videos of your gaming skills for others to enjoy. The more popular your videos are, the more views you get and the more cash you earn. If you enjoy gaming and Roblox, give it a go!

Head to the gaming shop to upgrade your microphone quality. It's important to always improve the stuff you create and record to boost your subscriber numbers. Making a video involves doing some fun on-screen activities. You can then relax and see how many people like your video!

Your avatar has energy, mood and hunger levels. Try to top these up because you'll be a better video-maker if these levels are full. Open a chest with the cash and gems you receive. Inside this loot, there may be a new WiFi router that'll really help you reach more people!

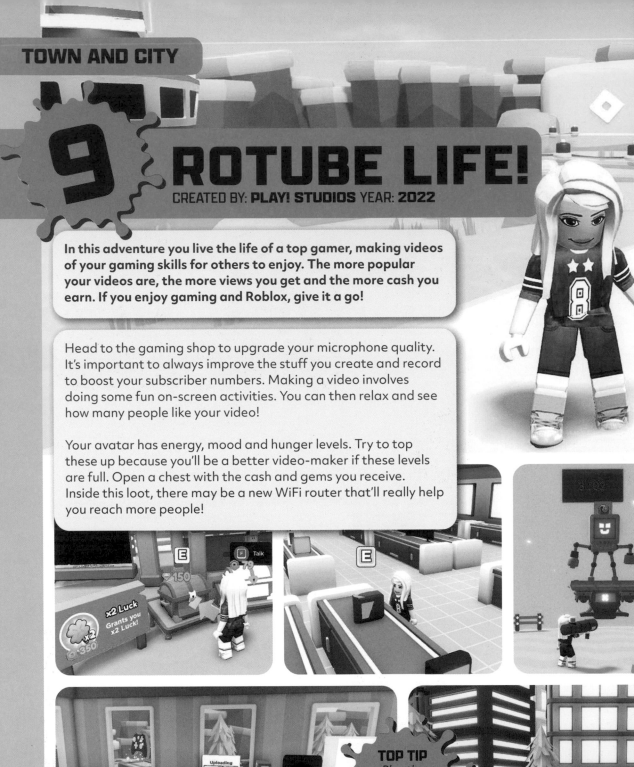

TOP TIP
Play the tutorial and earn 150 gems!

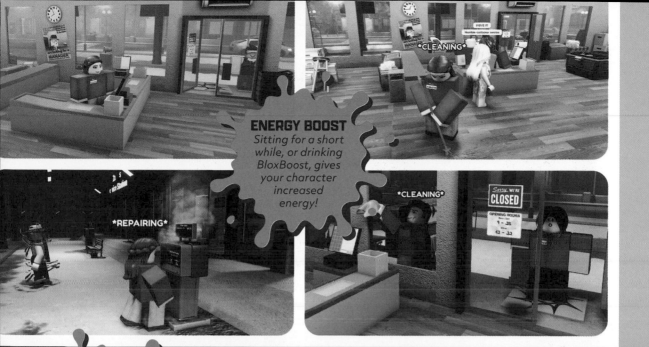

REPAIRING

CLEANING

CLEANING

CLOSED

10 ZACH'S SERVICE STATION

CREATED BY: **BLOX STUDIO** YEAR: **2022**

All cities need good service stations to keep vehicles running and motorists happy. Zach's Service Station is a busy place, with workers on duty round the clock to keep cars fuelled up and on the road! You'll earn money for keeping the business in good shape.

- Trash Bag (1 / 2)

As a service station clerk, make sure your energy is at max level so that you can sprint over to deal with drivers' requests. Refuelling cars at the pump, washing windscreens, cleaning stains and emptying trash bags is all part of a hard day's work in this city!

Employees need to keep an eye on the station's bills. Use the laptop to order more store stock and fuel for the pumps, plus looking at the ad monitors rewards you with ad tokens. Spend your earnings wisely in the shop as you look for upgrades and events to take part in.

SWAT

11 JAILBREAK

CREATED BY: **BADIMO** YEAR: **2017**

Choose the role of a good police officer or a sneaky criminal in Jailbreak – both are packed with adventure! Jailbreak reached six billion visits in 2023 and Roblox fans can't get enough of the action, drama and chaos it creates. It's classic cops versus robbers!

Busting out as a prisoner is not too tough. Look for keypads and keycards to open prison doors, fences to climb or crawl under and secret tunnels that set you free. On the outside, it's time to get really bad and commit robberies. This makes you a wanted criminal and an instant police target worth a big bounty!

The bank is a great place to rob. It has different levels and tasks and if you can dodge laser alarms and reach the vault, the cash will flash up in your inventory. The best tip is to team up with other criminals to get maximum rewards from the bank, and to make it harder for cops to catch you.

The new Crew Battles mode lets groups of Jailbreak players band together in fierce battles. When the action starts, the race is on for the criminals to complete their robberies before the police can arrest them. The best Crew Battles teams get the top rankings.

Police have lots of items and tricks to help them succeed. Officers spawn with weapons and handcuffs, they can use the map function to track movements and players with a bounty of over $2500 will be sent to the maximum security prison island. Being a cop is tough but exciting!

HIGH RISK
Flying with the jetpack item is an awesome way to escape from police!

12 BIG CITY TYCOON

CREATED BY: **READY, SET, MORE!** YEAR: **2021**

Get a fix of town and city, role-playing and money-making tycoon with Big City! It's an easy and addictive game that you'll want to share and play with your friends. Start out with a simple beginner house, sell lemons outside and get money flowing in to make upgrades to your city life.

Keep the helpful red arrow option on. It takes you to the objects you can afford and you'll soon see items, walls and equipment added to your house. When your house is completed, the progression menu lets you teleport to the next mission – creating a pizza restaurant in the city!

Add extra pizza ovens to earn more money and build the pizza shop successfully before splashing $5,000 on an apartment studio. Be patient when you buy things and get the stuff that will grow your business. Then add flashy furniture and paintings when you can afford it!

DRIVING FORCE
If a car is locked, just ask the owner to let you in!

13 WASHIEZ

CREATED BY: **WASHIEZ** YEAR: **2021**

In this town, the target is all about getting your car cleaned! Customers earn coins by taking vehicles through the car wash and staff get rewarded for running the wash and the shops around the map. The more you wash, work and clean, the more you collect skill!

Quests are updated each day and completing these tasks gives players extra cash. They're usually very simple, such as visiting a store or spawning a car, so make sure you tick each quest off for some easy money. Houses and offices are not cheap so keep the bank balance boosted!

Away from the chaos of keeping cars clean, Washiez gives you the chance to create luxury houses and offices. The build system lets you add your own furniture and decoration to the buildings, giving you the freedom to express yourself. Don't relax too much inside your home ... the cars need cleaning outside!

LIGHT UP
Keep lights on in buildings so you don't get a surprise in the dark!

14 REDCLIFF CITY

CREATED BY: **REDCLIFF CITY RP** YEAR: **2021**

There are lots of life choices to make in the Redcliff City game. Right from the start, you can click on the peaceful or loud settings. Redcliff is a city with lots going on, plenty of shops and buildings to enter and usually a bit of danger too!

Once you've spawned a house, there are some rules to follow. Keep it locked, otherwise robbers will be free to take stuff from it. Use the nine security cameras to properly guard the place and look out for fires being set. The emergency services are very busy in Redcliff!

The game gives you constant warnings about what's going on, including whether the city bank has been robbed (the new laser alarm is tough) and if criminals are on the run. Use any of the free vehicles to get around and parachutes were even added in 2023. If you're on foot, use the sprint function for a quick boost!

Central Ave

15 HAPPY LAND

CREATED BY: **MAKEHAPPY** YEAR: **2021**

Want to feel happy? Explore the Happy Land game and that's what you'll be! The idea is to tour the city, create a cool-looking avatar and do lots of fun stuff like build a career, make a home and drive awesome vehicles. The game reached 300 million visits in just over a year!

Maybe you'll work as a teacher, a doctor, a firefighter or a DJ in Happy Land? New users get an instant $100 reward and $20 for every five in-game minutes. Use the money to unlock land and cars, or maybe pick up a friendly creature in the pet shop. Grab a cute penguin for just $100!

Some top tips for new players include limiting the speed on your car to make driving easier, using the free bloxy radar item to track other players and buying the cheap $8 house so you can start a base. Interact with the Happy Land residents and check out the amusements and rides!

16 MAD CITY

CREATED BY: **SCHWIFTY STUDIOS** YEAR: **2017**

Mad City and Jailbreak (pages 24-25) are similar. You choose your role at the start and players can be police, prisoner … or an epic Mad City hero! The superhero section is something Jailbreak doesn't have, and most Roblox gamers take this role at first because it's so dramatic and thrilling!

As a hero you're ordered to use your powers for good. From the superhero lobby you must select the suit to take and special abilities to adopt. Titan, Hotrod, Inferno, Frostbite, Vanta, Voltron and Proton are the heroes and each has a slick move, from speed to fireballs, and teleporting to flying.

Take out your phone to check the status of missions and challenges. The reward for doing these is XP and cash, which gives you weapon upgrades in the shop. If you want to be a prisoner, switch roles and make an escape from the prison camp. Slipping through underground vents is the perfect way.

CASH COUNT
Save up your cash because some items and weapons cost millions!

Cover distances by spawning a vehicle. A Camaro car is a speedy option once you get used to the handling. With powerful items you can begin to loot the city, pick up daily bonuses and see your XP rise.

If you are police, hero or prisoner, always look for top tricks to help give you the edge. For example, use the shot jump move that flings you into the air when you fire, and always know the cooldown time after heists happen. Stay on top of the Mad City news to help you rule at your job!

17 COOK BURGERS

CREATED BY: **SSSQD** YEAR: **2019**

FRIENDLY FUN
You can set up your own server for free, so you and friends can play together!

Cook Burgers has over 350 million visits because it's a unique town and city game. Apart from grilling and frying food as a chef, there's no other job to focus on, no cars to ride or homes to furnish. Sound boring? Once you get flippin' the burgers, you'll see what fun it is!

Customers sit down and place specific orders, which the chefs need to cook. Pick up a plate and head to the kitchen. Keep an eye on the main screen showing all of the orders and the time left to cook them. If ingredients run out, use the machine to stock up on bread, meat, cheese and lettuce.

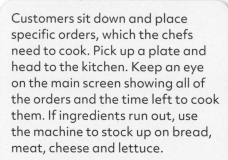

Earn plenty of cash for keeping customers happy, but get the orders wrong and you'll get less money. Simple stuff. Oh, and watch out for rats running around in the restaurant – these horrid creatures are very bad for business!

18 SEABOARD CITY

CREATED BY: **SHARK FIN STUDIOS LLC** YEAR: **2020**

Seaboard is a pleasant urban space where you pick a property, select a job, make friends with your pet and do lots of other interesting activities. When you arrive, check the city's population on the board in the main square – beginners might find it easier in a town with fewer residents.

Seaboard is by the coast, so why not tour the beach, Celebrity Cove or even Billionaire's Island? Create a home in Seagrove, Hills or Mountain estates. The mansions to choose from are impressive and you can change the colour of the walls and floors, or add a pool and security system.

Seaboard City has some fun twists that make it different to other town and city platforms. In the area where you spawn, there's the option to make your avatar a baby, a teen or an adult. Step on the baby button and you'll instantly shrink and have to crawl along the streets!

ADVENTURE

Adventure games are packed with action, epic missions, and loads of fun to keep your Roblox avatar entertained. Take a look at the very best games from this awesome genre – try them out once you've read loads of the tips and tricks!

DUNGEON QUEST

GARTEN OF BANBAN

FOOLS BEWARE
A popular adventure game called Doors added a super hard mode for one day only, on April Fool's Day!

BUILD A BOAT FOR TREASURE

ARCANE ODYSSEY

DRIVING EMPIRE

19 BUILD A BOAT FOR TREASURE

CREATED BY: **CHILLZ STUDIOS** YEAR: **2016**

Build your ship and set sail for your adventure! It's a perfect summary by Build a Boat for Treasure game developers Chillz Studios! Visitor numbers are well past three billion and with tens of thousands playing at a time, this game is sailing on as a Roblox classic!

Enter your build area and use blocks to create a ship that's ready for launch. Ships can be simple designs that actually look nothing like a boat, or huge creations that could dominate the water! Bigger is not always better, though. Just make sure it floats well and has good protection.

Why does a boat need protection? Because in this game, boats and teams of builders can come under attack from other players! Weapons blocks, like the mini gun and spike trap, can be used to damage other boats. Life can be dangerous out there on the water!

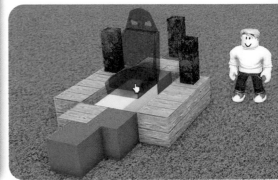

There are seven colour-based teams in Build a Boat for Treasure. Working in a team instead of solo mode means players can launch boats together. Each team has one leader and a team that must build together and decide when the vessel is ready to launch. Make sure the share mode is enabled, so you can pool blocks together.

Completing the game's quest function rewards you with gold and blocks. These random missions can involve tasks such as transporting certain blocks, finding and clicking on a block or even scoring a goal with a giant soccer ball! These are all fun ways to boost your resources.

OPEN CHESTS
Locate or buy chests and pocket the gold inside!

20 SONIC SPEED SIMULATOR

CREATED BY: **GAMFAM X SONIC** YEAR: **2022**

Be just like videogame superstar Sonic as you speed through stacks of amazing worlds, collecting rings and chaos orbs on your lightning-fast dash. Pets, limited time events, special Sonic skins and loads more extras are up for grabs in the quickest encounter ever to hit Roblox!

Rebirths, quests, adventures and stat boosts are all on offer. Your special moves include the spin dash charge, homing attack and boost. Use them at the perfect time to propel yourself along the course. Sonic's friends, Tails, Knuckles and Amy are all unlockable characters!

Sonic Speed Simulator developers Gamefam are experts in creating cool Roblox content. The clever group of game makers are behind more than 30 titles on the platform, including Car Dealership Tycoon, Weapon Fighting Simulator, Easy Obby and Hot Wheels Open World. Check 'em out!

SPEED SPIN
Enter the free spin every four hours to earn 1 million XP or 750,000 rings!

21 EVADE

CREATED BY: HEXAGON DEVELOPMENT COMMUNITY
YEAR: 2022

An adventure game with a big serving of horror as well! In Evade, the countdown starts by placing you in a random world. You must compete objectives before the evil Nextbots track you down and wipe you out. Run, hide, work as a team – whatever it takes to keep the adventure alive!

Complete objectives to buy items and utilities. The most helpful utilities include a radio, the radar and a decoy for fooling the chasing Nextbots. A flashlight or a lamp is also good to have, because when the darkness takes grip the chances of survival drop!

Evade has plenty of twists and turns to make sure the frightening fun never stops. One random person can be the Impostor for a short while, which grants a weapon and some protection from Nextbots. Deployables are special abilities that include barriers, teleporters and warning beacons. Join in and try to avoid being caught!

22 DUNGEON QUEST

CREATED BY: **VCAFFY** YEAR: **2018**

542/917

If you like adventure games with fantasy, magic, combat and levelling up, then Dungeon Quest is for you! Solo or in teams, you take on dungeon dangers and boss enemies, equipping yourself with superior weapons if you succeed. Harder dungeons open up to you as well.

Mages are magical fighters who deal damage from a distance. Their weapons and armour carry spell power. Warriors are more heavy-duty combat masters, with healers and tanks making up the rest of a Dungeon Quest team. Each has an important role in defeating enemies.

Get to know the desert temple dungeon. It's the opening location with a maze-like layout and rooms that will spawn the sand peasant mobs. Wipe out their HP and eventually you'll face the sand giant boss. Become a hero with your weapons and abilities to spend as much time as possible beating the bad guys!

RARE FIND
Abilities, armours and weapons rank in rarity from uncommon to ultimate!

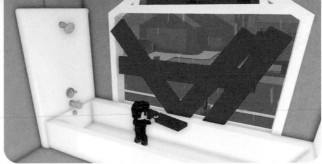

23 BREAK IN

CREATED BY: **CRACKY4** YEAR: **2019**

Some adventure games are loaded with mystery, drama and thrills ... welcome to Break In! This is a journey where a storyline develops, you explore scenes and follow orders inside a house. Events will happen beyond your control and when the baddies show up, take action to keep surviving each day!

You'll be guided through five days of action, with attacks going on at the house and scary things happening in the dark! It's all great fun, though, and staying clear of the villains is a skill you soon learn. Start your quest in the role of a kid (best for new players) before trying the adult role, where you protect others.

In-game badges are available for making progress. These can be simple achievements, like finding valuable items or turning on lights, or harder tasks such as the gold medal for finding the secret ending. Break In is an adventurous experience that's worth risking!

24 ISLANDS

CREATED BY: **EASY.GG** YEAR: 2020

Islands has more than two billion visits, making it a huge Roblox experience! The game is based around crafting items, collecting and harvesting resources, building, trading … there's even combat and fighting to master. Fans of Minecraft will love this special place.

BIG ACHIEVER
In your Islands profile tab, see how many achievement points (AP) you can collect!

The action begins on a small island. You have basic materials at first and a good task is to cut down a tree using your axe. You can then craft a wooden pickaxe and collect grass blocks. Build the grass blocks across to the next island. Your simple start will soon spawn greater tools!

Always look for ways to upgrade. Boost your simple workbench to the next tier, using wood and iron ore in a recipe. At the wheat farm, you can harvest the crop and plant wheat seeds. Actions like these can form part of your quests, which are seen in your quest journal.

Hold down to keep the red box within the fish zone   Time Left: 6

The level of materials needed, such as stone and iron ingot, to craft items are detailed in the crafting grid. During your missions you'll rack up coins and XP, which then help you obtain new items and higher status in Islands. You'll want to teleport to the Hub area and begin trading.

Be on guard for mobs! As well as being a fantasy-filled arena and a relaxing place, Islands also has some dangerous mobs that threaten you. Pirates, hounds, golems and crabs will get in your way, so tread carefully on mob islands. As a bonus, there's always the chance you'll find rare loot when you are fighting!

25 EXPEDITION ANTARCTICA

CREATED BY: **PLAYDUO STUDIO** YEAR: **2018**

Your mission is to travel across the dangerous snow and ice to reach the South Pole! This epic adventure is a very popular Roblox experience as gamers face glaciers, icebergs and mountains on their tricky trip to the bottom of the world. Be brave and good luck out there!

All expeditions begin at base camp. Find your way to base camp 1, then camp 2 and 3 before finally reaching the pole. Watch your energy and hydration levels and don't get lost in the wilderness. The best way to reach your destination is by following the poles in the snow along the route.

Each time you get to the South Pole, your expedition count increases. The more experience and success you have, the more your skill rank rises and you can unlock flags for your backpack. Visiting camps also gives you coin rewards. Getting to the South Pole earns 1000 coins!

Expedition Antarctica has an achievements system, ranging from easy to medium, hard and pro. The pro rating is earned for missions like getting to the Pole 25 times, making the trip without losing health and completing the tough journey in under 20 minutes.

Need more handy hints to help survive this snow-packed place? Jump instead of walk when you're on icy ladders, use the radio to communicate with other players and activate the checkpoints at each camp to save your progress. Also, collect water, energy bars and emergency flares at every opportunity!

TOP TIP
Toggle the camera view between players in your game to pick up tips from other explorers!

26 LEGENDS OF SPEED

CREATED BY: **SCRIPTBLOXIAN STUDIOS** YEAR: **2019**

Like Sonic Speed Simulator on page 38, Legends of Speed is another whirlwind race with a stash of rewards! As you dash through courses, collect orbs that grant you gifts called steps. Gems can also be picked up and going through hoops gives you big bonuses. Navigate the fastest route to victory while also pocketing items on your way!

TOP TIP
If you are at a high enough level to rebirth, you can collect rewards and gems as well.

Running courses are found in zones such as snow, magma, space and desert. Look out for speed ramps to fling you across the ground. Time a jump perfectly when entering a ramp and you'll go even faster. See you later, slow-coaches!

Check the leader board to see how your sprinting matches with others in your server. The top runners could have a million-plus steps, hundreds of hoops and taken part in over 50 races. Keep upping your pace in Legends of Speed to reach such impressive levels!

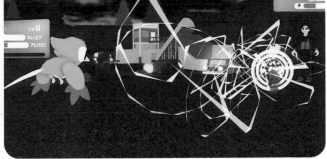
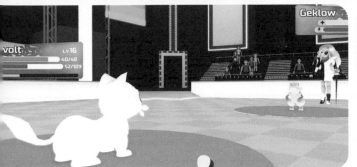

27 LOOMIAN LEGACY

CREATED BY: **LLAMA TRAIN STUDIO** YEAR: **2015**

Loomian Legacy is an adventure game with a fun story mode. Loomians are a cute type of animal that can be trained, traded and used in battle. This experience is not always fast and frantic, which means you and your friends can relax and enjoy the story-based journey.

The Loomians come in a variety of shapes, sizes and types. There are currently more than 200 of them, including air, electric, ice, water and fire, and each of these have an attack and defense rating. The entry-level Loomians include Embit, Dripple, Fevine, Eaglit, Vambat, Snocub and Weevolt. Cool names!

Follow the mysterious on-screen instructions to begin your adventure. You'll interact with your Loomian father, have combat tests early on, discover the Stone Tablet and be guided on a tour that will really challenge your brain and muscle power. There is absolutely loads to enjoy!

28 DRAGON BLOX

CREATED BY: **G RBLX GAMES** YEAR: **2019**

Dragon Blox is a type of adventure game involving lots of combats and duels. Take on top fighters and raise your rank. Your skill level is very important because it allows you to face tougher opponents. Are you brave enough to take on this challenging Roblox experience?

Think of skills as tools to help you overcome enemies. Each has an energy cost, damage and cooldown time. Energy blast, energy bomb, meteor punch, hellzone grenade and solar flare are all examples of effective skills in the dangerous world of Dragon Blox!

The more you defeat mobs and bosses through successful combat techniques, the more higher rating you will earn. When your power reaches a certain level, forms become unlocked. Forms (transformations) are types of fighters rated on their health, energy, punch and power level. Super Seijin is a basic form, but Super Seijin 15 is super tough!

Dragon Blox also has the option of visiting different levels, in the Crimson World and Planet Droid. Interact with the teleportation NPC to reach new realms and worlds – places like the Crimson Castle and the Nemba Base will present new challenges!

Need to step away from the screen for a short while? Dragon Blox has a clever mode called auto combat, through the AFK (away from keyboard) function. Activate this and your character can carry on fighting, even if you're not doing anything with the controls!

QUICK MOVE
The instant teleport skill only has a 15-second cooldown. That's much quicker than many other skills!

29 DRAGON ADVENTURES

CREATED BY: **SONAR STUDIOS** YEAR: **2019**

Mixing dragons with powers, quests, building and role-playing, Dragon Adventures is an epic ride – you even get to fly with your mythical companions! With over 500 million visits already and regular updates and season changes, there's lots to keep you coming back.

Follow Rodger, your guide, to get started. Choose to ride with a Rocircus or Saurium dragon and learn how to fly, fight and search for items. Beginner dragons such as these two have a lower speed and health rating. Dragons can breed too, so watch out for mysterious eggs and 'things' hatching!

Dragon Adventures has daily and weekly missions and as you try to unlock new worlds with your dragons, such as Undercity, Grassland, Jungle and Volcano, you'll soon learn how to be a hero. Raise your XP, keep your health (HP) strong and see how far you can journey!

30 ARCANE ODYSSEY

CREATED BY: **VETEXGAMES** YEAR: **2019**

Arcane Odyssey is getting better year after year as the developers add new levels, modes and quests. The game gives you the chance to explore the sea on classic ships, capture islands, build castles and become famous … or infamous if you join fights and start mischief!

Players also roam the land, looking for objects, food and items to place in their inventory. You can even dig for buried treasure! On the water, be careful that smaller ships are not troubled by deep seas and look out for castaways stranded on debris. There's always something to spot in Arcane Odyssey!

Other gameplay elements include trading goods, interacting with characters, finishing quests to pick up XP and mastering weapons. Never go near a pirate ship because they attack weaker opponents! If you can sink a pirate ship, you'll be granted treasures in return.

TOP TIP
Looking for buried treasure? Inside scroll charts are treasure charts with directions to find it.

51

31 WORLD // ZERO

CREATED BY: **WORLD // ZERO** YEAR: **2019**

The developers tell you to "go on an epic adventure" when you load up the hit Roblox game World // Zero. Select your starter class and begin a journey through one of many different worlds. Battle bosses, unlock classes, locate special loot and upgrade and equip your avatar to succeed!

As you increase your XP and level status, your character tier can rise to dual wielder, guardian, paladin, spirit archer and beyond. Master the slash primary attack move, plus the crescent strike, leap slash and dodge. Remember there's a cooldown time after each of these.

Check your daily, weekly, world and side quests. These could be defeating enemies, reaching certain levels, fighting in the PvP arena and rescuing villagers. Complete these and XP, chests, tradeable items and other goodies will reach your inventory. The world is at your feet in World // Zero!

AWESOME AWARDS
World // Zero is so good it has even won two official Bloxy Awards!

Kazoru
Legendar
(Click un...

Vegita

Inosoku

32 ANIME ADVENTURES

CREATED BY: **GOMU** YEAR: **2021**

Can you summon powerful heroes and assemble a top unit to save multiple worlds? This sounds tough, but once you spend time in control of Anime Adventures, you'll soon be bashing the bad guys and pocketing precious gems to build your super squad!

First you need to know how to summon. Each summon requires 50 gems and when actioned, a new fighting character joins. Fighters are ranked in rarity class, going from rare to epic, legendary, mythical and secret. Mythical and secret are incredibly difficult to spawn, though!

In the opening story mode, you venture through Planet Namak and will face the bosses Zarbo, Goldeo, Zezoom, Vurtor, Gunyu and Freezo. Provide XP units to your team to boost power as you secure victories against waves of enemy moves. Work as a top team!

33 YOUR BIZARRE ADVENTURE

CREATED BY: **BIZARRE STUDIOS**® YEAR: **2019**

The name is spot on – getting familiar with this game can be a little bizarre and take time at first! The aim is to build up elements called stands, which are strong and unique spiritual abilities. Stands are obtained by getting pierced with an arrow or merging with part of a rib cage skeleton. Bizarre, huh?!

SPEED BOOST
Unlock agility in the skill tree to boost sprinting speed and dashing distance!

There's also a storyline running in the game, which must be completed in the correct order. Visit the Giorno Giovanna character at the airport to get the opening story quest. Quests can offer rewards such as cash, cosmetics, experience, items and even change your stand.

You need to navigate the complicated skill tree too. There's a character, fighting style and stand tree. Routes in your character's tree become unlocked when you have enough skill points. Agility, vitality, worthiness, health regen and sturdiness all have a path. Just start playing Your Bizarre Adventure and it'll soon make sense!

LV. 2   LV. 3   LV. 4   LV. 5   LV. 6   LV. 7

10/20

34 BEN 10 SUPER HERO TIME

CREATED BY: **CARTOON NETWORK GAMES** YEAR: **2020**

Be like the TV cartoon hero and play a bunch of fun minigames! You can become a powerful alien and use out-of-this-world skills to explore and conquer Ben 10's awesome world. Load up the Omnitrix and see where the action and adventure takes you.

The Omnitrix is neat wrist tech that captures alien DNA and makes you become a different creature at the touch of a switch. Interact with characters like Grandpa Max and Kevin 11 as you tour the hero lobby. Become Grey Matter, a small frog alien, to slip through tiny gaps or use Heatblast's fire to burn a trail!

This Ben 10 game also has other amazing Cartoon Network mini adventures. Join Teen Titans Go! and be like Robin as you collect XP and zoom around a city, or see what's going on with the Gumball crew. The game's always being updated with all the latest TV cartoon adventures!

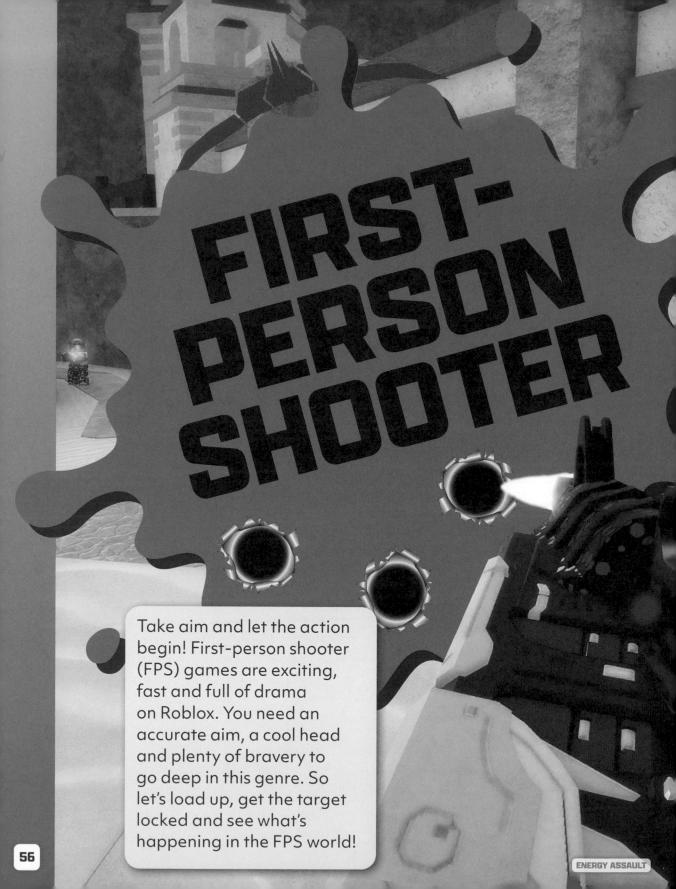

FIRST-PERSON SHOOTER

Take aim and let the action begin! First-person shooter (FPS) games are exciting, fast and full of drama on Roblox. You need an accurate aim, a cool head and plenty of bravery to go deep in this genre. So let's load up, get the target locked and see what's happening in the FPS world!

ENERGY ASSAULT

BAD BUSINESS

4 8 11 100
BIG PAINTBALL

-70

ISLAND ROYALE

AIMBLOX

Capture! (55)

TYPICAL COLOURS 2

35 ARSENAL

CREATED BY: **ROLVE** YEAR: **2015**

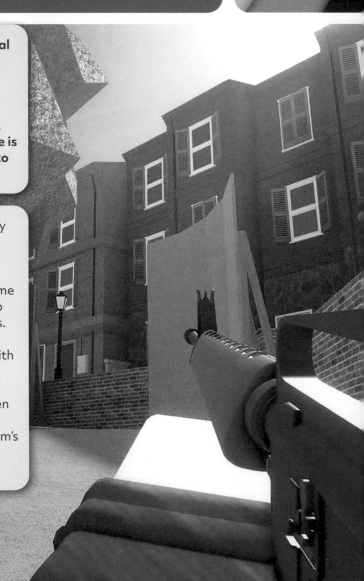

Spawn into an Arsenal battle and the pace is fast and the action relentless! It takes bravery and quick thinking to survive in this slick FPS arena. With a mighty range of weapons, including melee, pistol, rifle, machine and sniper options, the choice is immense. At first you'll just be happy to hit the target and last a few minutes!

In the standard mode, the aim is to stay alive so that you can eventually make an elimination using the crucial golden weapon. As you get your hands on different equipment, pocket the in-game currency (called battlebucks) and keep your fighter looking fresh with fun skins.

The top Arsenal gamers are brilliant with the 'aim down sights' option activated. This gives you a target on screen, meaning you can be very accurate when firing and really make the most of your weapon and ammo. Be aware of an item's reload time, though, as this leaves you open to attack as you wait.

Need some help to boost your battle skills? Just select the 'spec' option to safely spectate on a game. Scroll through the surviving players and take a look at their tactics, firing and in-game abilities to pick up important tips. A great option for Arsenal beginners!

Arsenal has more than 70 special badges to collect, depending on your success in the game. These range from simple awards such as making your first elimination, to insanely tough tasks like making a kill while only having a one health rating. More badges equal more power!

BIG CALL
When you are wiped out by a player, look out for them leaving their 'friendly' calling card on the screen!

36 COUNTER BLOX

CREATED BY: **ROLVE** YEAR: **2015**

ROLVe Community are awesome on the FPS stage! This developer knows exactly what it takes to excite fans, and Counter Blox is a fierce tactical battle with so much to keep you coming back. It's attack vs defence in a 5 v 5 arena, with danger hiding around every corner.

The counter-terrorists face up to the baddies. For the good guys to win, they must wipe out the enemy or defuse the explosive device that can be set by the other team. The maps on offer span the globe and give both teams lots of places to surprise their enemies from.

Trade weapons to boost your survival chances and spectate on other players to pick up tips and ideas. Customise skins and reach new tiers, using the cash you earn to bolster your avatar. Counter Blox is bursting with FPS thrills – keep the enemy in sight and don't let your team fail!

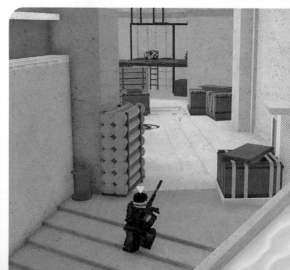

37 BAD BUSINESS

CREATED BY: **BAD BUSINESS** YEAR: **2019**

Keep locked on the enemy and support your team in Bad Business. Thousands of gamers can be on the server at the same time, showing what a popular place this is. Alongside your teammates, move through the map with accuracy and rack up the points and credits needed to progress.

Bad Business has some cool modes. King of the Hill tasks teams with taking and controlling an area, while Hardpoint is another map-based territorial tussle. Before deploying, select your loadout from one of the five options and be comfortable with your primary, secondary, melee and equipment choices.

Take some time to see the stats for your primary weapon. Fire rate, magazine size, mobility and damage power are all important to check. During a dramatic 15-minute event, you need as much control at your fingertips as possible. The more joy you have, the higher your XP, credits, prestige and level status will be!

TOP TIP
Hit the randomize button to switch up your loadout choices before a battle!

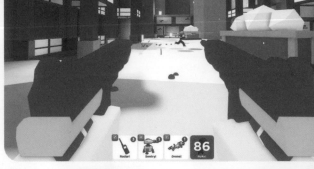

38 BIG PAINTBALL!

CREATED BY: **BIG GAMES™** YEAR: **2019**

For a FPS Roblox adventure with a colourful twist, check out BIG Paintball! In this game you need to be quick and accurate with the colourful pellets that fire from your weapon. The plan is to splash other players, called tagging, and earn better and more powerful weapons. It's easy to understand ... but tricky to master!

Some FPS games are highly technical and require a deep understanding of weapons and tactics. Not so in this title! Either in a team deathmatch (TDA) or free-for-all (FFA) battle, just point at an enemy and get them covered in colour. Earn credits to unlock superior weapons so that you can boss the battleground like a pro paintballer.

Players begin with the default, semi-auto weapon. This is lightweight and has a medium range. The default shooter fires only once per click, making it slow in a shootout. Upgrading to a faster fully-automatic item means you will blast the crazy coloured pellets at a dazzling rate!

Maps offer a different mission. Ranging from a mall to concrete, a safehouse and an abandoned nuketown, be careful as you sprint through the streets and fields. Look all around you for danger and when you see the coloured missiles filling the sky, take cover and try to eliminate the source!

Achieve winning streaks by hitting targets and earning BIG Paintball victories. As an incentive to succeed, abilities are granted depending on the total tags you have. Rewards include a turret firing ability called a sentry, plus a radar device that helps identify enemy players.

SPECIAL SENTRY
The powerful armoured sentry ability uses a special minigun with awesome impact at long range.

39 FOAM FRENZY

CREATED BY: **TEAM INTEL** YEAR: 2021

Much like BIG Paintball! on the previous page, but with foam blasters instead of coloured splats! Your job is to tag the enemy in one of the many maps and rack up a winning streak of eliminations. This game is full of foam and is very frenzied – the name is perfect!

Join the blue or the red team, choose a map and get going with your blaster. You could be in the woods or a city centre, but wherever you spawn use natural or man-made objects for cover and don't forget to climb ladders to fire foam on the enemy from high above.

Upgrade your primary and sidearm weapon to give you greater power. Bigger weapons will increase the range you can strike from and will give your XP level a huge raise. Pick up cash to spend on items in the shop and always be prepared for a nasty aerial nuke attack from the opposition!

QUICK TIP
Enable the auto sprint function to help you cover the ground quickly.

40 ISLAND ROYALE

CREATED BY: LORDJURRD YEAR: 2018

Island Royale is an amazing FPS ride, with plenty of other elements thrown in. It's a classic battle royale adventure with a mastery of weapons needed. Plus the building and survival skills take this to a whole new level. Drop from the skies and hope to be the last player standing!

Game modes include Solos, Squads, Duos, Zone Wars and Box Fights. Have close-range and long-range firearms to hand and begin collecting resources the moment your boots touch the ground. If you don't take out your opponent, they will react and end your time on the island.

If you play in a team or with friends, work out the roles you will carry out. One of you can rush the opposition while others provide cover, or you could task a certain player to track down chests and items. Always keep your weapons close at hand to stop sneaky attacks!

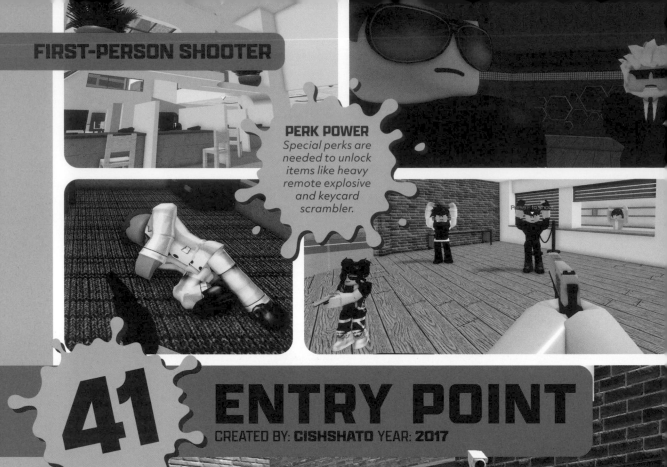

PERK POWER
Special perks are needed to unlock items like heavy remote explosive and keycard scrambler.

Press F to shoot

41 ENTRY POINT

CREATED BY: **CISHSHATO** YEAR: **2017**

Entry Point mixes FPS with crazy criminal adventures. There are lots of missions to take on and as a proper baddie, your aim needs to be perfect as the police and NPCs are there to raise the alarm and stop you from stealing and completing your quests. Once you start Entry Point, there's no way back!

Press V to knock them out

The best way to succeed here is by not attracting attention. Firing a loud weapon will turn heads, but using a clever concealed item is a much smarter move. Entry Point also has a Shadow War PvP mode, offering a quick match or full squad deploy.

Entry Point has many challenges to overcome. Guards, cameras, NPCs (non-playable characters), alarms, alerts and dangerous SWAT teams are all part of the gameplay. Act quickly and decisively and shut down attacks against you in seconds. Always have your FPS brain fully switched on!

42 FLAG WARS!

CREATED BY: **SCRIPTLY STUDIOS**™ YEAR: **2019**

FPS games are not just dash and destroy-type encounters. Flag Wars! sees players digging into enemy territory, searching for their rival's flag and then taking it back to their own base. What makes this a classic FPS title is the bunch of brill weapons and items available to help with the mission!

With the red or the blues, enter the action and begin the crucial quest to snatch the flag. Protect your teammates on daring raids and equip yourself with the tools needed. Shovels, trowels, drills and dynamite are just as important as your mighty rifles and SMGs!

Unlocking high-grade weapons instantly boosts your FPS powers. The Uzi is good in close combat, but switch to a sniper to cut out danger from a distance. Have two items you like using in two of your inventory slots and learn to switch quickly between them.

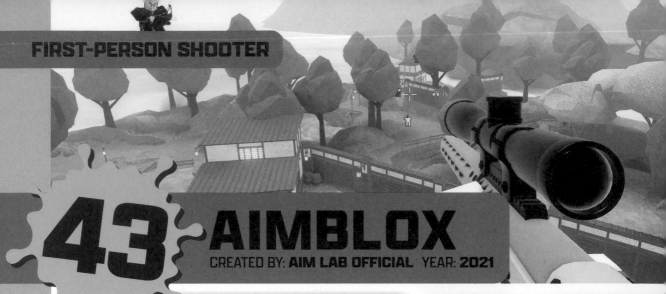

43 AIMBLOX

CREATED BY: **AIM LAB OFFICIAL**   YEAR: **2021**

Make sure you visit the sharp-shooting world of Aimblox. Even if you're not a big FPS fan, this game will probably make you one! Select Arcade mode for random fun like the space snipers event, or click on Competitive for team battles that will test your reflexes and instant aiming.

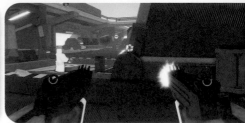

Aimblox offers player versus player (PvP) or player versus environment (PvE) experiences. Take on PvE and you'll come across all sorts of solo missions and quests against NPCs or machines. Follow the tutorial instructions and you'll know exactly where to sprint to and what to shoot at.

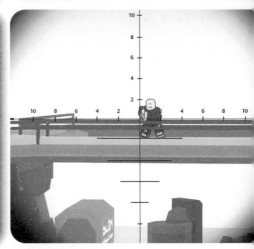

The good news is that Aimblox lets you set the difficulty rating. Select easy, sweaty or epic level depending on your ability and click the hardcore mode to on or off. After a few days exploring the maps and bases, you should feel confident to crank up the pressure for a proper test of your FPS skills!

44 ZOMBIE UPRISING

CREATED BY: **USSF** YEAR: **2020**

SOUND ON
Keep the sound on for this game – you'll hear the zombies approaching before you see them!

Sometimes in FPS games, things will get a bit gruesome. That's just what happens in Zombie Uprising! It's not a difficult game to understand – just get your items ready and blast the hordes of horrible creatures that stumble your way on screen!

You begin in normal mode, before you reach level 10 and can unlock hard and then apocalypse mode. Automatic and semi-auto weapons are the best, allowing you to plug the zombies at speed and zap their power. The beasts can quickly make up ground though, so keep on your toes!

With exclusive battle passes and perks, daily missions and plenty of awesome items to obtain, your sharp shooting is soon rewarded. Make sure your character stays in good health because if you're a decent fighter, the boss enemy will appear after the rounds and really cause you some damage!

45 PHANTOM FORCES

CREATED BY: **STYLIS STUDIOS** YEAR: **2015**

Phantom Forces is one of the prime games in the FPS genre. Packed with detail, drama and team-based action, it keeps you coming back for more! Upgrade your abilities and become a top team member, as you explore loads of maps and hunt down the opposition.

You can join the blue ghosts team or the orange phantoms. When you spawn, head out with your weapon ready and target any rival who scans on your horizon. Don't scatter fire too much, because you'll soon drain your ammo. Each time you reload, your weapon has less ammunition to launch.

Phantom Forces is very technical, but try not to get too baffled and stick to the basics! Once you're more advanced, you can pay attention to primary and secondary weapon slots, item lists, KDR values and all the other hi-tech stuff. Just rack up eliminations and you'll be well-respected!

[+10]   Squadmate spawned on you

Gamers have a chance to vote for a map choice. These include fun terrains like Crane Site Revamp, Desert Storm and Highway Lot, plus there are fighting modes such as King of the Hill, Team Deathmatch and Capture the Flag.

Unlocking weapons is key. Soldiers do this by gaining XP and boosting their weapon unlock rank. You'll soon master the short and long-range tools needed and learn how to stay hidden, before dropping in to surprise the enemy team. With plenty of practice, you'll be an expert fighter as the clock counts down each match!

TOP TIP
See where the sneaky opposition is firing from by the coloured trails their ammo creates in the air!

46 ENERGY ASSAULT

CREATED BY: **TYPICAL GAMES**   YEAR: **2021**

Called a 'futuristic FPS' by makers Typical Games, this experience uses electrical energy machines to zap the opposition through a fun range of game modes. Team up with the reds or the blues and zip through the scenes looking for a lethal shot to lay down the oppo!

BEST BADGE
Want to prove you're the best? Claim the MVP (Most Valuable Player) award in a match by achieving the highest score!

Energy Assault games last for 10 minutes – although getting through 10 seconds can be tough at first! Learn from the more experienced players on your team, hang back and hide before popping out for clinical strikes. This may seem sneaky but it's the best way for new players to survive.

Hill Control is a popular game mode. A team takes a point for every second they control the hill zone. Artefact is a similar mode, with a point awarded for each second a teammate has the artefact object. Keep your radar, ammo and hitmarker HUD signs switched on to help you win!

47 TYPICAL COLORS 2

CREATED BY: **ROLVE** YEAR: **2015**

Taking inspiration from the Team Fortress 2 game, Typical Colors 2 (TC2) is another quality FPS stage that's well worth a visit. With more than 100 unlockable weapons, the red and green teams clash in a series of duels. Pick a colour and make your mark!

Payload is a testing sequence to take on. One team must push an explosive in a cart, while the other tries to stop them in their tracks before the time runs out. Use your ammo wisely and base your tactics around reaching the checkpoints. The cart also has regenerative powers for the players.

Make every shot count, especially with single-fire weapons that have a slow reload time. Poke out from rocks, buildings and trees to cause maximum impact and make yourself a difficult moving target by leaping and moving from side-to-side. You need every trick in the book to get a victory!

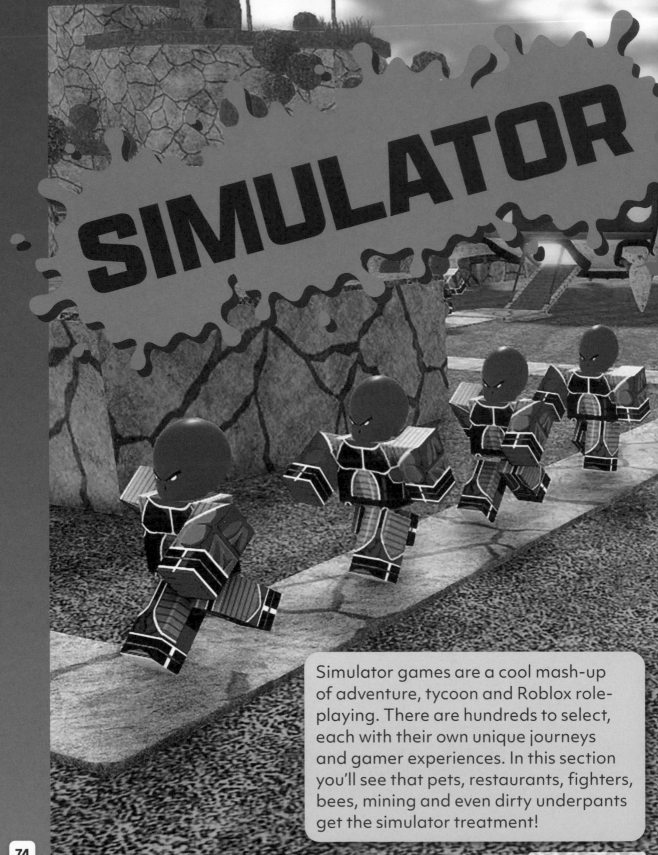

SIMULATOR

Simulator games are a cool mash-up of adventure, tycoon and Roblox role-playing. There are hundreds to select, each with their own unique journeys and gamer experiences. In this section you'll see that pets, restaurants, fighters, bees, mining and even dirty underpants get the simulator treatment!

PILOT TRAINING FLIGHT SIMULATOR

UNBOXING SIMULATOR

Crazy Unboxer

↓ Finn's Supplies Shop

Supplies
Shop →

FISHING SIMULATOR

DESTRUCTION SIMULATOR

+4 → 0
+4 XP/0 XP

Search..

AVATAR CATALOG CREATOR

75

48 PET SIMULATOR X

CREATED BY: **BIG GAMES PETS** YEAR: **2021**

Collect pets and diamonds and enjoy a brilliant adventure with **Pet Simulator X**. The action seems endless as you wander the spawn world and lots of other zones via teleporting. Use your creature friends to help you mine all the goodies and see your gaming level rise along with your coin and gem count!

Mining items in the spawn world will pocket you a lot of rewards. This can be done by walking around, but try to get your hands on a cool hoverboard to speed things up! Boards can be obtained by spending Robux or through completing quests.

Pet Simulator can be a relaxing journey, but most gamers crank up the pressure and take on the mastery missions to boost their level. Collecting lootbags, using potions, hatching eggs and breaking coin piles and crates are just some of the activities connected with the mastery.

23.19k

94

Empyrean Fox
Epic

Once you have a million diamonds to your name, you can unlock the trading plaza at the back of the spawn zone. It's an expensive place to gain access to, but inside you can use special trading machines, enter unique areas and take part in pet auctions. Work hard in Pet Sim X and the rewards are awesome!

As well as covering the ground, don't forget to launch yourself into the air in Pet Simulator X! Step on a springboard to catapult to the clouds, then carefully bounce through to reach new lands or limited time events and pick up rare rewards. Luckily, if you fall down from the sky you won't be eliminated.

Purchase to Unlock

6.27m

2.16m

57.5k

9   8

FREE SPREE
Free gifts are unlocked every 10 minutes – make sure you redeem them!

SHOP

David

49 MY RESTAURANT

CREATED BY: **BIG GAMES X** YEAR: **2019**

This fun sim game challenges you to build a restaurant, keep the customers fed, collect cash and create a bigger and better place to eat. It's great to play for five minutes or five hours! Begin by seating a customer, taking their order, cooking on the stove and then taking their money.

With money in the bank, make hiring a cook and a waiter your next move. This speeds up the ordering and food prep stages. As the cash racks up, buy more seats, chairs and stoves to keep your restaurant busy and successful. Add more floors to really build your empire!

Higher grade staff can be unlocked when your level rises. Outside of your restaurant is a sign showing how many customers you've served. Tour through other players' places to see what their business are like. By unlocking more tasty recipes, you'll attract high-paying visitors and even VIPs!

TOP TIP
When you level up you'll get extra cash, cooks, waiters and more great items!

Emerald Pickaxe

A strong pickaxe to get you rare materials

⏣ +12   ⌛ x4

💲 3,100

TRADE OFF
Mine more than five million blocks to open the trading function.

Stone
1

Molten Stone
1,960
💲 1

50 MINING SIMULATOR 2

CREATED BY: **RUMBLE STUDIOS** YEAR: **2022**

Time to dig deep, Roblox fans! Get your tools out and start mining for precious ores to sell in Mining Simulator 2. You'll get coins, eggs and more top treats in return. The most successful miners collect billions of blocks, millions of eggs and have over 100,000 coins stashed away!

Your default wooden pickaxe has just a +1 power and x1 speed. Ditch this early on and upgrade to metal, which has +4 power. Your collected objects go in your small backpack, but with just a storage level of 5, swap this for a 30-level large backpack.

Ores range in value. Copper has a base selling value of $25, but silver is $120, ruby is $575 and diamond fetches $5,500! You need to equip the expensive super drill tool, with +65 power and x28 speed, to access this mineral. Mining Sim 2 needs quite a bit of play time to make the cash needed!

Dirt
1
💲 1

51 LAUNDRY SIMULATOR

CREATED BY: **DEV HOUSE UK** YEAR: **2021**

Did you think doing the washing and taking care of dirty clothes was just for boring people? Join Laundry Simulator and you won't want to stop! It's one of the simplest games on Roblox as you collect items and place them in the machine. The fun comes when you build up your own laundromat.

Touch a vacant plot to claim it, collect items from the conveyor belt and stuff them in your washer. Putting them through the chute gives you a basic rate of five coins. Be patient as you collect coins that can be spent in Archy's shop in the main lobby.

Upgraded washing machines have bigger capacity, quicker times and better multipliers. Make sure you also buy a more effective basket; the 500-coin green basket has auto grab and a 20-item capacity. With plenty to spend Robux on, such as nitro speed and plus 50% capacity, Laundry Sim keeps you in a spin!

Inventory: 9/75

Equipped: 3/3

Dr Dolphin

Killer

Goldar III

Booth

STAT CHECK
Check your in-game stats to see the yen earned, stars opened, raids defeated and many more successes!

Boothead

Bighead

Bighead

Bighead

52 ANIME FIGHTERS SIMULATOR

CREATED BY: **SULLEY** YEAR: **2021**

It's tricky to say exactly what this sim experience is all about. Obviously there's a BIG slice of fighting action, plus crafting, training, upgrading and exploring. It's not a typical sim game, but with 'simulator' in the title, Anime Fighters is worthy of a place in the genre!

You control a loyal group of fighters, who you must send to attack a range of enemies and bosses. They set about zapping the foe's HP and when beaten, a victory rewards you with yen, the in-game currency.

Move through the worlds as you win battles and pocket cash. When you're fighting in worlds 10 and beyond, you know you're well on the way to being a pro anime hero! Interact with NPCs and quests, move quickly by accessing mounts, raise your level from noob to hero and boss the battlefield. Good luck!

LVL 11

-67

53 SWORD FIGHTERS SIMULATOR

CREATED BY: FULLSPRINT GAMES   YEAR: 2022

Similar to Anime Fighters Simulator, Sword Fighters Simulator sees you battle against enemies, with every sword swing and victory giving you better weapons and items. The game only launched in 2022 but soon raced to nearly 200 million visits in under 12 months!

Equip the best weapon you can and make regular visits to the upgrades shop to use your collected coins and powers. Unlock eggs to pick up helpful pets along the way. Goblins and orcs are easily defeated in the opening rounds, but be on guard for fierce rivals in future worlds.

Fighters can forge ores to craft stronger elements, harness pets to multiply power gains and boost swing speed, walk speed and damage multiplier. Cash in on the daily spin chance each day you play – a luck boost, coin reward or some star dust will be very welcome!

54 ALL STAR TOWER DEFENSE

CREATED BY: **TOP DOWN GAMES** YEAR: **2020**

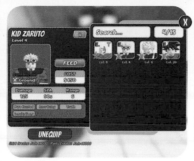

Mix simulator action with fighting and tactical combat in All Star Tower Defense. Your objective is to summon a team of heroes, all with unique skills, and equip them for an all-star offensive. As you prepare to enter world 1, get ready for attacks from every angle!

At entry level, heroes Zaruto, Koku and Koro have different damage and range powers. Enter Story Mode, transport to the battlefield through a pod and begin placing your units in the best positions to fend off waves of enemies.

Units will need upgrading as soon as you can, as more powerful baddies swoop in. You can upgrade your heroes during battle to make the most of new attacks. As the brains behind this battle, get all you can from your team to become the best all-star defender!

WEIRD WORD
As you teleport, your transporter might 'frobulate'. This is how it works out the coordinates you want to travel to!

55 BEE SWARM SIMULATOR

CREATED BY: **ONETT** YEAR: **2018**

Collect pollen from the flowers and make lovely honey from it. What could be simpler? If that sounds like a dull game, just load up Bee Swarm Simulator and join the millions who love this 'sweet' experience. The bees act as your best buddies here and are with you all the way!

Hatch bees by claiming a hive, then place an egg in a honeycomb cell. Take the bees to a nearby field and instruct them to zap up the powerful pollen. Watch your backpack's honey meter rise – with this loaded up you must then return to your hive. It's so easy and addictive!

Time to boost your honey levels by visiting the shop and buying a faster scooper, more bee eggs or a larger backpack. Eggs can be basic, silver or gold. You can even transform your bee into rare, epic or legendary status with the royal jelly item.

Bee types boast a range of abilities and strengths. Just activate their powers by collecting tokens that they spawn, plus you can combine abilities to make a mighty bee swarm! Bees are rated by their energy, speed, attack and the rate they take in pollen and produce honey.

One of the biggest threats is from scary mobs and monsters that lurk in some flower fields. If they attack, you'll lose all the pollen stored in your backpack. You won't be able to fight them, but luckily your bees can step in to protect you. These buzzing insects are awesome friends!

BEAR-ILLIANT!
Interact with the bears around the map. Complete the quests they set to earn more honey!

New Type Discovered!
You hatched a...
Cool Bee!
Blue Rare
A sarcastic bee who's a little better than the others. Sometimes boosts pollen from Blue flowers.

TELE TASK
The teleport power costs 400 Robux, but it's such a cool ability!

56 BUBBLE GUM SIMULATOR

CREATED BY: **RUMBLE STUDIOS** YEAR: **2018**

Getting coins, gems, eggs, pets and epic items all comes down to one thing in this sim experience – blowing massive bubbles with bubble gum! The more you blow, the more you collect. You can even jump into the clouds and discover awesome new worlds and adventures.

You start at the regular bubbler level, but soon hope to reach novice, expert, extreme, bubble master and beyond. Your level rises by blowing big bubbles, hatching eggs and finishing bubble pass missions. Trading also unlocks once you've opened 3000 eggs.

Be patient when you start making bubbles. Pocket 400 coins to buy the extra stretchy gum that will boost your bubble size from 25 to 100. Special titles, potions, hats and abilities will all come your way once you blow up bigger and better gum creations. Keep on blowing, folks!

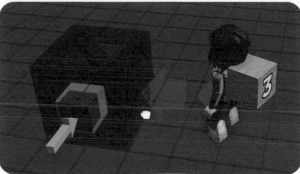

57 FACTORY SIMULATOR

CREATED BY: **GAMING GLOVE STUDIOS** YEAR: **2021**

Simulator, building and tycoon genre fun is all mixed up with this exciting game. In Factory Simulator you're tasked with harvesting resources and making items to create a business empire. If you fancy a challenging sim that's not all about pets and combat, then click on this!

As you go mining and refining in the lands around you, you need containers to store your collections and precious resources. Grab dropped goodies and always check back to your inventory area to upgrade your tools with the cash you earn.

It may seem tricky at first, but a little time spent in build mode will teach you the basics. The use of better containers and machines will boost your empire and raise your tier status. Plus, Factory Simulator will usually have events you can quickly teleport to for a fresh mining test!

58 BOTCLASH SIMULATOR

CREATED BY: **WILD EXPLORERS** YEAR: **2022**

If you've dreamed of sending bots to fight your battles and eventually take on boss enemies, you've clicked on the perfect Roblox game! BotClash Simulator is relaxed enough for a fun adventure, but still has epic robotic clashes that need your expert guidance.

Developers Wild Explorers call this a fight for humanity's last hope as your loyal machines stay by your side in simulated combat. The starter bots you command have limited HP and DPS ability, but higher-grade events unlock after regional bosses are defeated.

Bots can be unlocked in locations that include Lost Valley, Space Station, Frozen World and Desert Ruins. Get coins and gems as you level up and finish achievements. Bots come in rare, epic, legendary and mythical grade, so get the best you can to get the job done!

FRIENDLY FORCE
Have a friend playing on the same server as you to get a 10 per cent bonus to coin and gem income!

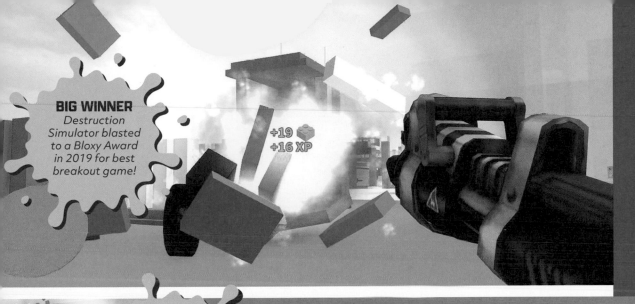

BIG WINNER
Destruction Simulator blasted to a Bloxy Award in 2019 for best breakout game!

+19 🧱
+16 XP

+10
+10 XP

59 DESTRUCTION SIMULATOR

CREATED BY: **SILKY_DEV** YEAR: **2018**

When a Roblox game carries a big warning sign at the start, you know something massive is about to happen! Don't worry, though, because the alert is just to tell you that because of all the explosions in this game, there may be a small lag on your device. Take cover for a destructive ride!

+3
+3 XP

25/25

Destruction Simulator is simple but great. Blow up and destroy as much of the brick-built environment around you as you can, using powerful rockets and bombs. Do this to pocket bricks and collect coins and rewards. Your level and rank will rise and you can aim at more challenging targets!

Backpacks can be upgraded to hold more collected bricks for you to sell. There's a magic carpet to fly you around the screen too. As you reach higher levels, jump on the automated paths to the north and south to quickly transport you to new zones. Point, blast and have a smashing simulator time!

60 CATALOG AVATAR CREATOR

CREATED BY: **ITSMUNEEEB** YEAR: **2021**

The prime purpose of simulator games are to give you a cool experience. Catalog Avator Creator does just that because it's a simple platform where you try on avatar items and looks for free. Giving your character a top appearance is so important in Roblox, so this is a genius idea!

Unlike in many other games where items and clothing cost money, you can craft completely new and fresh looks with just a few clicks. Accessories, hats, animations, bundles and loads more are all here. Play with your friends to really dress to impress!

If you want to spend, any Robux you splash out in-game will be saved to your inventory, so you keep the designs you create. Play with the freecam mode to take fun shots, add effects, explore community outfits and even search for a particular avatar you like to copy their costume. Hours of fun!

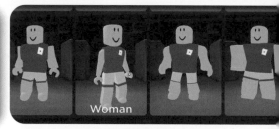

FISHING SIMULATOR

CREATED BY: **CLOUD ENTERTAINMENT** YEAR: **2019**

Chill out and cast your Roblox rod! Fishing may seem like a boring pastime to some people, but this simulator is so addictive and popular. Catching a range of fish, selling them for coins and upgrading your equipment is your main duty. Time to cast off!

You begin as a Learner at level 1, then progress to a Novice at level 5, then a Decent at level 10, before becoming a Seasoned Fisher at level 30. With a rod equipped, cast it in the water at Port Jackson island and keep the white line in the green area of the meter. It's easy and the fish will soon hook on!

Walk over to Caster at the docks to sell the fish for money. There are all sorts of species in the waters, from trout to stingray, with rarer creatures having a higher price. Finn's Supplies is the store to get tools from, Deckard's Boats has vessels to buy and the aquarium is the place to display any rare species that you don't want to sell!

EXTRA QUESTS
Don't forget to chat with Raygan at Raygan's Tavern to pick up extra quests.

62 UNBOXING SIMULATOR

CREATED BY: **UNSQUARED** YEAR: **2019**

Unboxing is a big thing – and that's why you should experience the Unboxing Simulator! Just go around bashing and smashing boxes and gifts to collect GOLD coins and games, unlock hats and take control of pets. It's a bit weird, but beating the boxes to discover cool stuff is worth the effort!

Once you've mastered the basics, there are all sorts of twists and special things to do. From teleporting to the wizard so you can access enchants, to finding locked crates that spawn in random places, this sim has plenty going on. You'll soon rise from being just a noob unboxer to a fresh unboxer and beyond.

Buy a stone hammer for 150 coins to help you unbox. Keep picking up cash to eventually reach 30,000. With this loot you can get a wave blade weapon – a fast category unboxer with x3 power! Costing just 1000 coins, unlock the castle area for added adventures as a new player.

BOX BADGE
Get the 'boxalicious' badge by unboxing a million boxes!

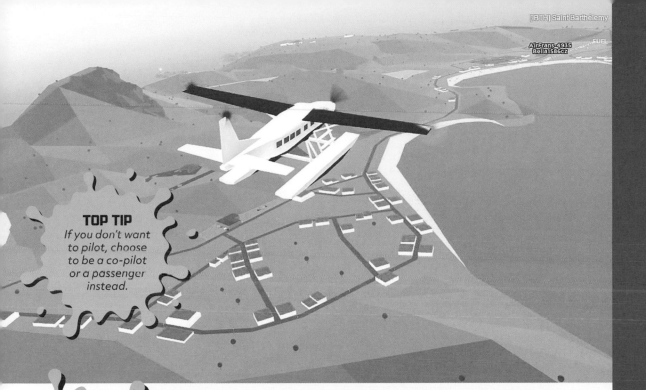

[BTH] Saint Barthelemy

AirFrans-4935
Bella1586cz

FUEL

TOP TIP
If you don't want to pilot, choose to be a co-pilot or a passenger instead.

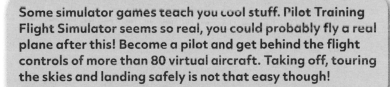

63 PILOT TRAINING FLIGHT SIMULATOR

CREATED BY: **ORANGE12345** YEAR: **2010**

Some simulator games teach you cool stuff. Pilot Training Flight Simulator seems so real, you could probably fly a real plane after this! Become a pilot and get behind the flight controls of more than 80 virtual aircraft. Taking off, touring the skies and landing safely is not that easy though!

Choose the map and airport to take off from, then a plane to board. Get comfortable with the controls and follow the yellow taxi lines to reach the runway. Line up correctly, then max the throttle and lift off for the clouds! Cruise at comfort and take in the scenery below.

Landing is the toughest part and usually takes a lot of practice. You'll need to touch ground before your fuel runs out and make sure your land speed indicator is engaged. Good luck taking the aircraft down and taxiing safely on the tarmac. This sim is one of Roblox's high points!

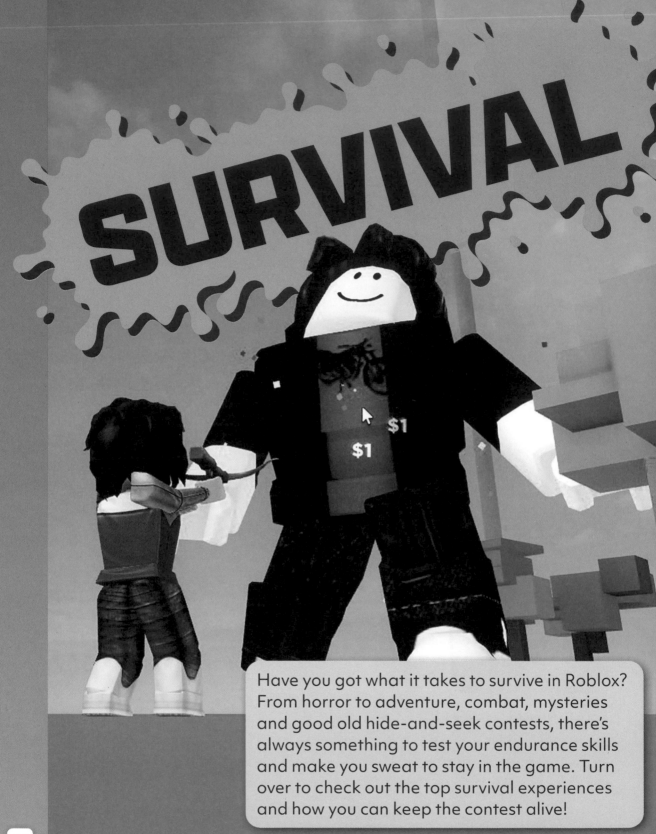

SURVIVAL

Have you got what it takes to survive in Roblox? From horror to adventure, combat, mysteries and good old hide-and-seek contests, there's always something to test your endurance skills and make you sweat to stay in the game. Turn over to check out the top survival experiences and how you can keep the contest alive!

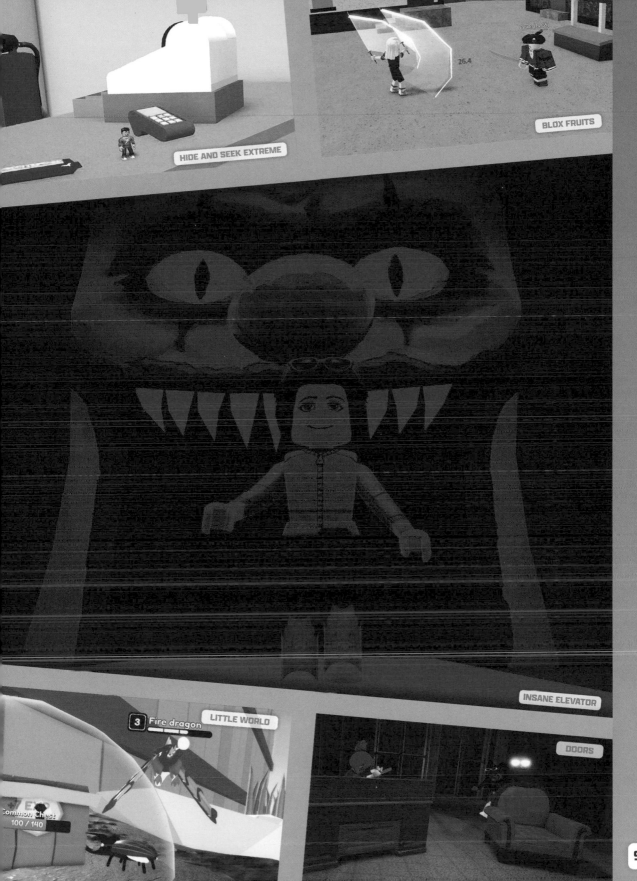

HIDE AND SEEK EXTREME

BLOX FRUITS

26.4

INSANE ELEVATOR

LITTLE WORLD

3 Fire dragon

DOORS

Common Chest
100 / 140

64 SHARKBITE

CREATED BY: **ABRACADABRA**   YEAR: **2017**

Whether you're playing the original SharkBite, or SharkBite 2 from 2022, it's a scary adventure as you try to survive in the water. When the countdown finishes, the shark or the players will be the winner. It takes nerves and a good command of your boat and items to survive this ride!

You will mostly be picked as a regular player when the game starts. Your chances of being nominated as the shark are usually very low. Select your boat, cruise the water and avoid being snapped up by the giant fish below you. Use your tools to reduce the creature's HP.

Different shark species will be released, although just one each round. Each has a different speed, health and size rating. The shortfin mako is quick, but has very poor health (HP). The great white is bigger and boasts more starting HP. The mighty orca is an apex predator with max health, size and stacks of speed!

Upgrading boats and weapons is very important. The bigger your boat, the better protection you have from shark bites! Combat boat and cruise ship is the ultimate, but you'll need to collect lots of shark teeth to reach that level. Weapons are graded on an accuracy and damage scale.

If your vessel is smashed by the shark, you'll find yourself scrambling and swimming in the water. Head for any floating pieces that will give you some protection from attacks and be aware of your oxygen level if you drop below the surface.

DAY BREAK
The game moves from day to night. In the darkness it's much harder to spot the predator!

65 DOORS

CREATED BY: **LSPLASH** YEAR: **2021**

Doors smashed the three billion visits mark in under two years – it's a huge survival, adventure and horror experience! As the game's name suggests, you have to venture through doors and solve the puzzles and mysteries in the rooms behind them. It can be scary, but also lots of fun!

The survival quests begin in the hotel. Find the key in reception to open door 1. Your target is to get beyond door 100 by being smart, cracking all the challenges and not being fazed by the boss enemies you'll encounter. That's right – behind some doors are creepy creatures to defeat!

The enemies, which are known as entities, include beings such as Rush, Ambush, Seek and Eyes. These try to slow your progress down as you search for doors. Entities can appear in more than one room, so look out for clues. When the hotel lights flicker, that's a sign of incoming danger!

66 GIANT SURVIVAL!

CREATED BY: **BIG GAMES™** YEAR: **2019**

Another huge hit from the BIG Games studio, Giant Survival! is technically a comedy genre experience, but it's all about surviving and staying in the game! You're challenged to evade and help destroy giant characters and progress through rounds and collect upgrades and items.

A random map, such as treehouse, factory or neighbourhood, is selected and the giant begins to roam. Use your beginner crossbow to fire at the huge mob and collect cash for every strike you land. The giant's health bar will drop until it is defeated and victory declared!

You can hide behind structures, get close for accuracy or stay clear of the giant's destructive footsteps. Look out for special game modes, like Double Giants, when there are two enemies to fight at once, and use your cash wisely to unlock new pistols and launchers.

67 BLOX FRUITS

CREATED BY: **GAMER ROBOT INC** YEAR: **2019**

The survival strategy in Blox Fruits is to live through battles with enemies and bosses, developing your fighting powers and upgrading along the way. Key to staying in the game are the blox fruit items. These mysterious fruits grant mega powers when consumed by Roblox players!

Blox fruit consumables come in three classes – natural, elemental and beast – with more than 30 varieties in the game. They can be earned by doing damage in raids, dealing the final blow to an enemy or collecting from hourly spawns plus trading, gifting and buying with Robux.

Fruits don't have regular names like apple and banana. Instead, falcon, ice, sand, dark, phoenix, dragon and spirit are some of the cool tags they have! Venture out across seas, be brave in duels and earn cash and XP for the risks you take. The survival quests in Blox Fruits are epic and exciting.

80 Evil Crabion

7 Fire dragon

68 LITTLE WORLD

CREATED BY: **COUNTER IMPACT** YEAR: **2019**

2 Fire dragon

2 Fire dragon

6 Fire dragon

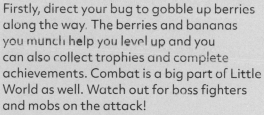

Usually if a game has bugs in it, that's a bad thing and it means it doesn't play properly. In Little World, a bug is actually a good thing because that's the character you start out as! Begin life as a little 'ladybug' and strive to survive in various zones as you explore, collect fruit and train hard.

Firstly, direct your bug to gobble up berries along the way. The berries and bananas you munch help you level up and you can also collect trophies and complete achievements. Combat is a big part of Little World as well. Watch out for boss fighters and mobs on the attack!

You'll need to reach certain levels to unlock quests. With minigames, daily rewards, pets, chests, houses and much more, Little World has so much going on for a little insect game! Vote for events that catch your eye, like obby rush and bug battle royale, to keep the challenges coming.

69 HIDE AND SEEK EXTREME

CREATED BY: **TIM7775** YEAR: **2015**

Many survival-based games involve a splash of scary stuff and jeopardy. Hide and Seek Extreme has loads of excitement as you dash to stay in the game, but it's not frightening at all. Your aim is to hide from the It character and survive until the clock runs down. Easy? Not always!

When the random map is selected – it could be a kitchen, bedroom, store or several other areas – the hiders then have one minute to sprint away and find a secret place. When It is unfrozen, their mission is to move through the map and find all the players. If you get caught, then you're out of the round.

The It person has some special moves to help them track the hiders. Glue spots put the brakes on the runners and the secret camera gives you helpful extra eyes. Watch the 'studs away' counter to see how near the seeker is. Don't get too close and keep moving until the end of the last the round.

GAME BOOST
Look for black squares and circles. These will blast you high and teleport you to a new hiding place.

70 INSANE ELEVATOR

CREATED BY: **DIGITAL DESTRUCTION** YEAR: **2019**

Makers Digital Destruction tell us there's a "99 per cent chance" we will fail at this survival game, but don't let that put you off! Insane Elevator is a cool and chaotic quest to see how many floors players can conquer. Hold on tight, because it's a ride full of ups and downs ...

HIGH TIMES
Need a boost? Pick up the jetpack item for just 24 Robux!

Step inside the elevator with the rest of the server's players. When the 'ping' goes and the door opens, step outside to face the enemy and bring the fight! Spend the points you earn for progressing on shop items like rocket shoes, torches, coils, speed potions and health boosts.

There's also a smaller, separate Roblox game called Insane Elevator Testing. Made by the same developers, it's simply a practice zone for new levels before they appear in the real experience. Have a go and see what could enter the full game in the future!

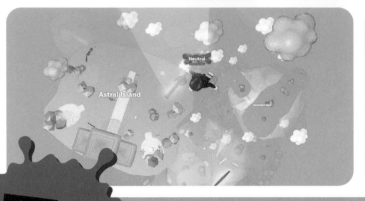

71 NINJA LEGENDS

CREATED BY: SCRIPTBLOXIAN STUDIOS YEAR: 2019

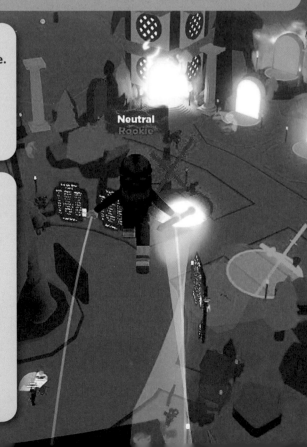

Scriptbloxian Studios have done a great job with this all-action fighting game. It's packed with features, drama, storylines, character progression and much more to keep gamers loading it up. The best ninjas will be the survivors who train, fight, collect new weapons and reach all the epic islands!

Swoop and swing your cool weapons, canes and swords to pick up ninjitsu and chi rewards. Trade in as soon as you can because superior items mean a superior ninja warrior. If you can, pick up the x 2 coins and x 2 speed boosts to really get you moving past your opponents!

As well as ninjitsu levels, your rank, streak and win count are also collected and shown on the leader board. As a new player you'll be desperate to progress from beginner rookie status! Take to the air too in Ninja Legends 2. Use the special trampolines and explore the skies for more battles and goodies!

72 NATURAL DISASTER SURVIVAL

CREATED BY: **STICKMASTERLUKE** YEAR: **2008**

One of the oldest Roblox games, but still one of the best! It's a battle to survive as a disaster heads your way on a remote island. Along with the rest of the players, you must make quick decisions on how best to ride out the danger coming towards you. Tense times!

When the random map is selected, you are teleported across from the lobby tower. There's a brief wait while the natural disaster sweeps in, which could be a flood, blizzard, sandstorm, fire or something else disruptive. Will you climb to safety, head inside for shelter or race across the island to dodge crumbling buildings?

Before the chosen disaster is announced, take a look at the conditions on screen to work out what it could be. This will give you a vital head start. Finding high ground is often a good solution, but remember that everyone else will be scrambling for safety too. In this game, survival means acting fast!

SOUND ADVICE
Listen out for danger. If a sandstorm is coming, you'll probably hear the winds pick up speed!

Disaster Warning:
Flash Flood! Seek high and stable ground

TYCOON

Look up the word tycoon in the dictionary and it says stuff about wealth and power in business and industry. In the Roblox world this is still the case, but tycoon also means fun, action and loads of top games! Find out what you need to be a boss player and reach your goals before the other top tycoon gamers beat you to it!

SUPER HERO TYCOON

Update Computer!
75,000 Subs

Unlock Silver Play Button
100,000 Subs

YOUTUBER TYCOON

ULTRA POWER TYCOON

TROPICAL RESORT TYCOON

CAR DEALERSHIP TYCOON

73 THEME PARK TYCOON 2

CREATED BY: **DEN_S** YEAR: **2012**

Get ready for a rollercoaster Roblox experience! Theme Park Tycoon has over one billion visits because it's such a great place to be. It mixes business tycoon fun with building tactics and roleplaying. As you create a wonderful park of rides, the cash in your balance will rise ... just like your rollercoaster!

Begin with a simple teacups ride to help you work out the tools and items. Each ride needs an entrance and an exit, plus a path to show paying customers where to queue. Open the attraction and set the entry cost. Don't charge too much for a ride because that will make it unpopular!

Add areas for your visitors to buy food and drink. Click on the stalls function to include these. This will help expand your park and pull in the numbers. Check on the feedback you get from customers – you can see their happiness rating and any thoughts they have.

Work through achievements you make, which give you in-game credits. This can include unlocking certain rides and attractions. The leader board will display players who've collected the most cash and had the most guests. The top Theme Park Tycoon players cash in millions!

As well as building your own rides, tour through other attractions to pick up tips and ideas. As you hope to build bigger events, it's a good idea to see how more experienced Robloxians set up their systems. You're not in direct competition with them, so get clues from the best theme parks around!

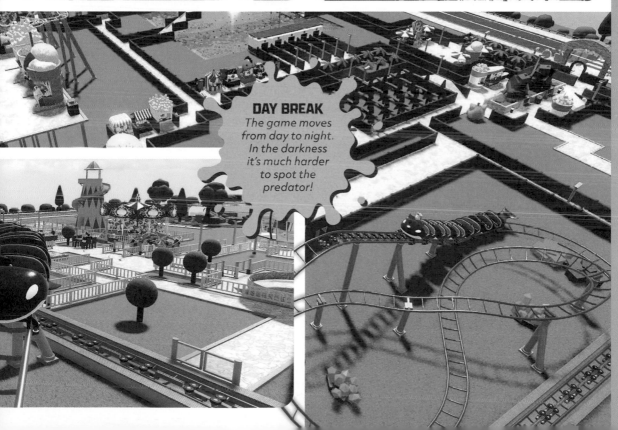

DAY BREAK
The game moves from day to night. In the darkness it's much harder to spot the predator!

Chair
$1,080

74 MEGA MANSION TYCOON

CREATED BY: **WILD ATELIER 2021** YEAR: **2018**

Tycoon games often involve great building scenes, allowing you to create a perfect home full of cool stuff! Mega Mansion Tycoon lets you build a cool house, too. Just follow the buttons on the ground and put up walls, floors, windows, doors and whatever else you want to construct.

When your creation takes shape outside, walk around inside and click the red buttons to add a couch, carpet, table, counter, paintings and much more. These items all come at a price. The more you play and build, the more your earnings and cash balance will rise.

Pick up your money by walking to your postbox at the start of your path. Mega Mansion Tycoon also includes awesome cars and vehicles. A parking spot for your home costs $25,000 though, so if you want a garage you'll need to save really hard. It's worth it in the end!

LIGHTS ON
When you add a ceiling it will become dark in your house, so have enough cash for lights too!

75 CAR DEALERSHIP TYCOON

CREATED BY: **FOXZIE** YEAR: **2018**

Rev your motor and put the pedal down in Car Dealership Tycoon! You're both a business exec and a racing driver as you build up an epic vehicle empire from scratch and race mega machines. Players collect miles and money for progressing – it's a dash to the top!

Choose your starting dealership and unlock the first $4500 daily reward. You can then use the cash to add walls, doors and a new platform to your dealership business. Only small cars will be available to you at first, but keep collecting and the cool sports cars will soon appear.

Your income will rise and remember to complete tasks to boost your wealth. The teleport tool lets you switch to new zones in a flash, including spots like the police, drift, dune, mountain and drag race tracks. Engine power upgrades, new body kits and extra customisation tools make this game a blast.

76 LUMBER TYCOON 2

CREATED BY: **DEFAULTIO** YEAR: **2009**

'Wood' you believe how much fun this tycoon game is! Act like a real lumberjack and use the wood and trees around you to create stacks of money and have a happy life. Lumber Tycoon 2 is a great mix of roleplaying and tycoon strategy. It's very relaxing and addictive to play too!

Collect wood from the map and sell it at the drop-off point to earn lots of cash. Items range in value, from cheaper elm, walnut and cherry to more expensive fir and pine. Sawmills turn logs into planks. Visit the Wood R Us place to begin your tree-tastic empire.

Interact with Ruhven in the land store to begin purchasing extra land, starting at $100. With the use of better tools, machines and vehicles, your earnings will rise steeply and you'll be a boss lumberjack in no time. It's hard work in Lumberland, but stick at it for a fun tycoon time!

77 ULTRA POWER TYCOON

CREATED BY: RAINBOW FLOWER STUDIOS YEAR: **2021**

Unlock special powers and take on powerful enemies! This may not sound like the usual skills for a tycoon game, but that's what makes this creation by Rainbow Flower Studios so great. Like Super Hero Tycoon, your mission is to be the best you can and build a business empire to crush others!

With the aim of one day being "the richest in the game" and having your name flagged at the top of the screen, select a starting power from the likes of hunter, cursed and dark flame. These have different hero abilities and tricks to defeat the other heroes ready to invade your business.

As your factory grows, keep stepping on the green button to pocket cash. Place down as many gen machines as you can, adding new levels and staircases to expand your gaming powers. When the supply crate countdown starts, rush outside to pick up the special items it will drop.

78 SUPER HERO TYCOON

CREATED BY: **SUPER HEROES™** YEAR: **2016**

Now you can become one of the universe's ultimate players! Super Hero Tycoon is a classic tycoon platform, mixed with the excitement of building up your empire and pocketing loads of cash. Who will you choose to control and what will your buildings look like?

At the start of your adventure, select your character. There are 10, including Superman, Spider-Man, Thor and The Flash. Just whizz over to that zone and claim it. Inside your new space, buy a dropper machine to earn cash. Walk over to the cash area and step on the plate to transfer your earnings. Simple!

Be patient to allow your bank balance to grow. Your hero will need upgraded dropper machines that earn more money. Also, begin building walls and add an extra floor and staircase to your tycoon factory. The bigger it is, the bigger your value in cash.

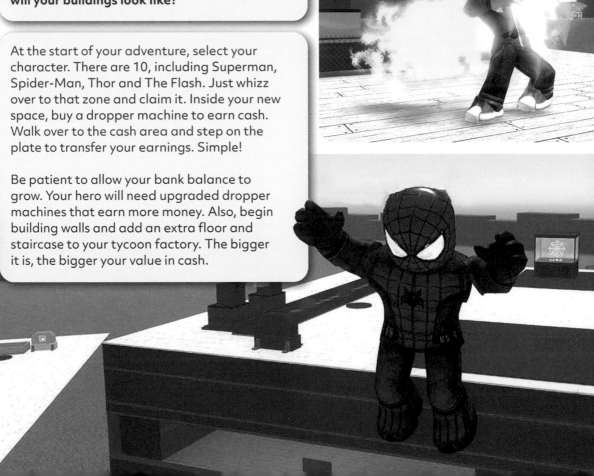

Hulk Swing

Buy Super Jump
$5000

Web Blast   Spidey Senses   Web Swing

Web Shooter

PACK PURCHASE
The robber pack allows a hero to steal others' weapons and cash.

Remember to arm the security door to your building, because you don't want intruders sneaking in and taking your stuff. Super Hero Tycoon has a weapons and abilities system, so be prepared for other heroes to attack you when you're busy working!

More walls, loadout pads, bunkers and turrets (those last two features cost Robux) will all make your building and business empire stand out from the rest. Raise your level by creating a high-grade factory and be clever as you do it. If you're lucky, the cash crate will boost you the maximum 1000 each time!

79 YOUTUBER TYCOON

CREATED BY: **SHINY PIXELS** YEAR: **2021**

Everyone loves Roblox and everyone loves YouTube. This game mixes both amazing worlds! The mission is simple: collect as many subscribers as possible and pocket money as you become famous as a digital screen star. The tycoon part of this game rocks too!

Claim your tycoon area, collect your first free dropper and you'll be ready to go. Step on the green button on the ground floor to keep banking the cash. Your first computer costs $100 and as you record and edit, your subs count rises. Add upgrades and new droppers to build your business.

As your percentage bar progresses and fills, you have the chance to rebirth. This takes away money and subscribers, but does give you a money and subs multiplier, so it's worth thinking about. Add new levels and new computers to see your YouTuber status rocket!

LEVEL UP
On higher levels you can add new workers to help you. The first worker costs $50,000!

80 TROPICAL RESORT TYCOON

CREATED BY: **READY, SET, MORE!** YEAR: **2020**

Some tycoon games are quite dangerous, with other players ready to steal your stuff or attack. Tropical Resort Tycoon is not like that. You head out for a luxurious time on a lovely warm island, building a place to live and work. Sweet stuff!

Walk to a front desk and set it up for free, then collect cash at regular intervals so you can build a cool hotel with walls, stairs, lounge areas and workers. Pay attention to the outside of your building too, adding a grand entrance, plants, fountain and more road. You can even expand the island for $1000!

Have the 'show buyable object' function switched on so you can always pick up items you can afford. You may want to save money at times, to buy more expensive things like roads and a golden cart. The currency you have and your net worth is on the leader board – the more you progress the better tycoon you become!

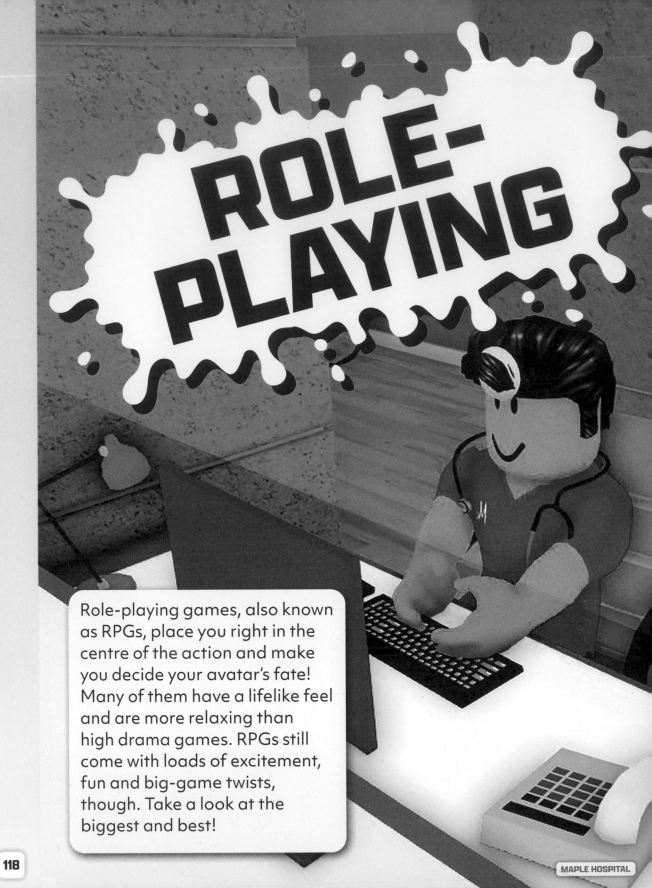

ROLE-PLAYING

Role-playing games, also known as RPGs, place you right in the centre of the action and make you decide your avatar's fate! Many of them have a lifelike feel and are more relaxing than high drama games. RPGs still come with loads of excitement, fun and big-game twists, though. Take a look at the biggest and best!

ROYALE HIGH

METRO LIFE

PETS AVAILABLE!

Wabbit
AGE: 0

CLUB ROBLOX

TREASURE QUEST

HEROES ONLINE

119

Royal Palace Spaniel

Newborn

81 ADOPT ME!

CREATED BY: **UPLIFT GAMES** YEAR: **2017**

Along with Brookhaven, Adopt Me! is the biggest role-playing universe to explore on Roblox! If you like to dress in cool gear, create a stylish house, trade with other players and act out a fantastic life, then join in. Oh, and of course you can adopt babies and pets too!

The nursery is where the adopting system starts. Choose to take on a creature or a little human. Pets can hatch from eggs, which need your attention because they want feeding and care at certain times. Simply tap the egg to stop it being hungry. Finish tasks to earn bucks so you can upgrade your Adopt Me! stuff.

On the family scene, decide to be a baby and get adopted or become a parent who will adopt. Your achievements and tasks will get bigger, but keep the animals or babies in your life happy and healthy. You'll spend hours in this place, along with millions of other gamers!

GREAT GIFT
Keep claiming daily rewards. On day five, you'll even pick up a small gift!

Newborn

HOSPITAL ENTRANCE

Maple Hospital

82 MAPLE HOSPITAL

CREATED BY: **MARIZMA GAMES** YEAR: **2022**

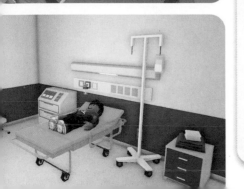

In just one year since launch, Maple Hospital reached 500 million visits! Roblox users clearly enjoy role-playing in a hospital and healthcare setting, which is very different to other popular RPG experiences. There's plenty to do at this hospital depending on the role you choose.

It may sound a bit painful, but be brave when you're inside the hospital and exploring the treatments, surgery rooms and systems. Your starting role can be a patient, nurse, resident or janitor. You need level 10 status for doctor or surgeon and a game pass to be a paramedic, security or hospital director.

Maple Hospital has a server size of 50 gamers, so it can be a busy place with lots going on. Use the elevator to visit all floors in the building and unlock doors to uncover secrets. It's a unique Roblox game, but as you learn more each time you play, the fun you have really makes it a top place to try out!

83

CLUB ROBLOX
CREATED BY: **BLOCK EVOLUTION STUDIOS** YEAR: **2021**

This amazing RPG game is considered to be a world of possibilities. That makes sense, because it's possible to role-play, enjoy minigames, adopt a pet or a baby, build a house and experience fun weekly events! Club Roblox is definitely a prime RPG place to check out.

When you begin, decide if your character's age will be adult, teenager or child. Adopt your first baby early on, either a boy or a girl, then give them a name and choose their behaviour type. This includes being calm or anxious, good or evil and introvert or extrovert. Pick wisely!

You can then take your new baby home (tap the teleport option as it's quicker!) and start customising your house. Create your dream-home look and keep your new family full of smiles. As you collect tokens, purchase cooler stuff and even a fun car to tour the town. Join the club and enjoy!

SWEET SUCCESS
Want a sweet move to make? Munch on tasty cupcakes and donuts at the new bakery building!

84 TWILIGHT DAYCARE

CREATED BY: NIGHTY STUDIO YEAR: 2021

When you role-play in Roblox, that sometimes means looking after young children and babies. Twilight Daycare, by Nighty Studio, is packed with exactly that, plus loads more jobs and options as a caretaker, parent, security or manager working in the healthcare industry. It's a fun but fast-paced place!

Whilst performing any one of the adult jobs, it's important to remember that the care of the little ones is the most important thing in Twilight Daycare – no kidding around!

You can also play as a young player, and try to look after your needs and make sure you're happy. Needs include feeding, sleeping, brushing teeth ... and going to the toilet! Luckily, as a toddler you can fulfil these needs by yourself and you don't have to rely on adult help. Interacting with baby toys and playing on fun rides are other important tasks.

85 METRO LIFE

CREATED BY: **HOUSE OF CREATORS** YEAR: **2023**

One of the newest Roblox RPG journeys, launched in spring 2023, Metro Life soon rocketed to having over 20,000 players online at any time. Mixing role-playing with city adventures, your task is to adapt to life in a vibrant seaside metropolis and build all you need for a VIP lifestyle. Nice!

Most of the role-playing is done through your mobile phone and its helpful apps. To explore the city, open the map and search for a location, or zoom out to see more of what's around. Tap to share your location and use the flashing arrows to guide you to exactly where you want to go.

Claim and set up your house, look for a free vehicle and drive around to see the sights. It's easy to add fun objects from your favourite job, including police officer tools and a doctor's medical equipment, plus you can also travel on the new metro system. Metro Life is totally relaxing!

TOILET TIME
All of the bathrooms in Metro Life are fully operational. You'll even hear the toilet flush!

ENERGY BOOST
Drink coffee from the machine for a quick energy boost!

86 ROVILLE

CREATED BY: **TEAM CRYSTAL!** YEAR: **2018**

RoVille is such a clever and exciting adventure. Like many RPG worlds, you must survive and progress each day, hoping to collect cash and boost the status of your home and car over time. Plus, your hunger, tiredness and cleanliness levels drop during the day and need attention. Look after yourself!

When your starter home is created and you've spawned a basic car, look for a job to get some money rolling in. There are chef, cashier and office jobs, but the high-paid work is more difficult. To earn cash for being a rocket engineer, pilot or archaeologist, you need to go to school!

At school, there are at least 10 tests and 10 school days required to gain your important graduation. Or, you can get an 'instant graduation' bonus if you spend 299 Robux! Everything about RoVille is slick and smart. Hang out and have a fun life here with your role-playing friends!

87 BERRY AVENUE

CREATED BY: **AMBERRY GAMES** YEAR: **2022**

There's lots to do in Berry Avenue for new and experienced RPG fans. It's a fab place to hang out, either with friends or other general players, and the instructions are easy to follow. The game's graphics and systems look different to other big role-play adventures, making it feel very fresh.

Reaching a billion visits in just over a year, the game's popularity comes from the range of roles on offer. Pick from being a good worker, such as in a bank, coffee shop or as a firefighter, or go rogue and be a criminal or a spy! Berry Avenue has lots of twists and turns and plenty of locations for role-players to live and hide.

Your home can look just as you want and keep an eye out for cool cars to hop inside. If you want a luxury limo you're gonna have to pay extra, though! With lots of entertaining items, missions and avatar customisation to choose from, the options for spending your time are vast. Take a stroll along the avenue and enjoy!

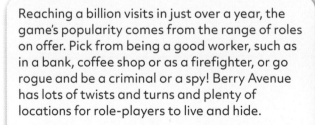

88 TREASURE QUEST

CREATED BY: **NOSNIY GAMES** YEAR: **2019**

Toxic bows, potions, scrolls, bosses, quests and monsters. If all this doesn't sound like a RPG-type game to you, then think again! Treasure Quest is tagged as a role-play adventure and even though there are no pets or babies to adopt and cute houses to build, it's still a big game in this genre!

The mission is straightforward when you start: just loot the top treasure being protected by evil monsters. You'll fight and blast your way through, beating down the monsters with your moves. Use your special whirlwind power to wipe out enemies, but be mindful of its cooldown time.

You'll get through to the boss monster and need one final big victory to claim the precious treasure. Coins and rewards will come your way as you progress. Rise to level 100 to access the pro lobby, use potions for a super boost and defeat an elite boss to pick up legendary loot. This RPG world is intense!

PIZZA PARTY
Call the Pizza Palace on your mobile and get a snack delivered to your apartment!

89 ROYALE HIGH

CREATED BY: CALLMEHBOB **YEAR: 2017**

This is your ever-growing dream world! Royale High is a place for stacks of RPG adventures as you tour places such as Diamond Beach, Fantasia Hotel, Sunset Island and of course the famous Royale High school. Join the millions of gamers who come here every single week!

Check your lesson schedule and attend your classes on time. Subjects include chemistry, PE, English and dance. You'll level up by going to your classes and earning high grades. The better you do at school, the more rewards you'll earn, so study hard.

Don't forget to do your homework on time and place it in the homework boxes by 3pm. Away from school, use your mobile to stay in touch with friends and have fun as you socialise and party after learning is over. If you get powers of 12 elementals you can attend the magical Enchantix High School!

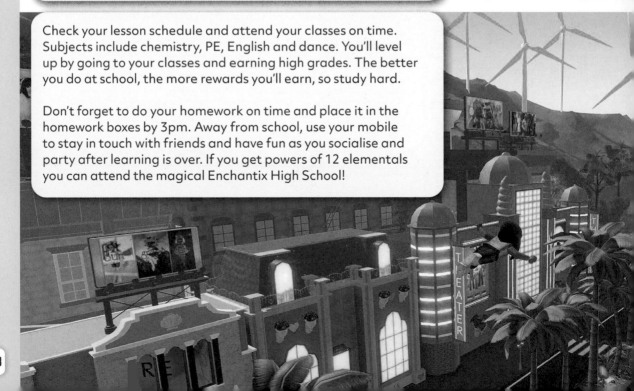

90 HEROES ONLINE

CREATED BY: **BLOXXIT STUDIOS** YEAR: **2018**

Bringing in brilliant bits of play from adventure and survival genres, Heroes Online puts you in the role of a hero fighting for justice or a villain causing havoc on the streets. Complete your quests, get level-ups and see your heroic character rise to the top!

When you go into battle as a goodie or a baddie, check your health, XP and stamina levels and keep the pressure on your opponent. Dashing forward and backwards, blocking and sidekicks are all part of your key moves. Heroes Online has over 100 abilities to unlock.

The quirk system is a big part of the game. These are like goals you need to achieve and, along with in-game quests, tick them off to get player boosts and greater powers. Quirk moves range from health drains to enemy smashes and even a cement trap. Get online to do them all!

OBBY

Roblox obstacle games are fun, exciting and packed with twists and adventures. Known as 'obby' games, they usually have lots of jumps, drops, precision walking and targets to reach. They can be bright and happy events or mix in scary plots and threats. Whatever you face in an obby, don't take your eyes off the screen or your fingers off the controls!

OBBY BUT YOU CAN'T JUMP

THE DROPPER

MEGA EASY OBBY

HOLE IN THE WALL

TEAMWORK PUZZLES 2

PLAY AREA

131

91 TOWER OF HELL

CREATED BY: **YXCEPTIONAL STUDIOS** YEAR: **2018**

In 2023, Tower of Hell reached 20 billion visits to make it one of the most popular Roblox experiences of all time! You need precise control pad or keyboard skills to climb the levels and complete obstacles with deadly accuracy. Just keep going higher ... if you can!

The timer starts and your adventure is instant. Jump gaps, reach tiny platforms and spaces and keep on the right path to reach top spot. The challenge just goes on and on and, guess what? If you fall, there are no checkpoints and it's back to the start. Aarrgghh!

You begin in Noob Towers, but for a totally tough time, enter the Pro Towers zone. Here, the obstacle danger gets even more difficult and the speed you must move and make decisions at is extreme. One wrong step and it's game over and you'll drop from the tower!

92 MEGA EASY OBBY

CREATED BY: **AUTHENTIC CREATIONS** YEAR: **2019**

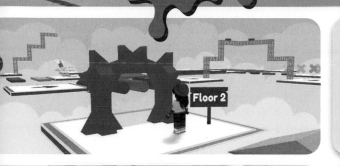

Roblox obstacle games are famous for being tough and annoying, but is this one really mega easy? Nope! The good thing is it's easy to get started and you'll want to keep playing and challenging yourself as you take on the parkour stages. There are over 800 stages to tackle!

In Mega Easy Obby, the colourful obstacles involve jumping on blocks, balls, bars, climbing steps, ladders and all sorts of tests. Pick up gems for finishing a stage and collect fun pets and extra items. As a beginner, just focus on taking the right steps and getting as far as possible.

Luckily, there is an easy mode option, which means the deadly lava will have no effect on you. Check your stage progress bar to see how far you've reached and don't rush things. It's always better to take a few seconds to work out the best moves and jumps to make. Enjoy the challenge!

SPECIAL LOOK
Use gems to add cool fire, sparkles or smoke to your avatar on the course.

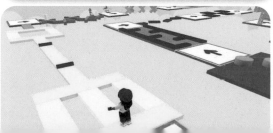

93 THE FLOOR IS LAVA

CREATED BY: **THELEGENDOFPYRO** YEAR: **2017**

If the classic game of escaping the rising lava isn't tough enough, this version adds obstacle challenges as well! When the clocks starts, don't waste any time in climbing to safety and jumping through the obstacles to beat the incoming red hot danger.

A random map will be chosen and the race is on to escape. Every other player will be speeding to reach high ground, so move quickly and get a clear view of the obstacle items. With over a billion visits, The Floor Is Lava is one of the top obby attractions!

Spending Robux is one of the quickest and easiest ways to progress and outrun the lethal lava. The ability to double jump, leap with a jetpack and fire a grapple hook to reach safety are huge bonuses to have. Play for two minutes or two hours, because this game is fun but frantic!

EXTRA OBBY
Look for the free bonus level obstacle course from the lobby!

94 SPEED RUN 4

CREATED BY: **VURSE** YEAR: **2014**

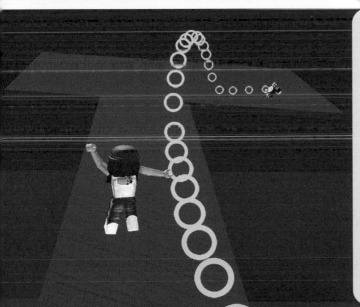

Get your speedy shoes on and dash and jump through the levels! This obby game is all about watching the clock and completing stages in the best possible time. Your avatar will leap and twist in a chaotic effort to reach the final part of each section.

Being quick is essential, but it sometimes pays to take a second to work out the best route to finish a level. There may be a shortcut or a sneaky direction to take. This will come with experience and the more practice you put in, the better Speed Run champ you'll be!

Speed Run also gives you reward badges for any spectacular deaths you may suffer! A toxic ending by nuclear waste and a cosmic death after falling into the vast space are just two of the badges given. The best advice is to stay in the game, though, and keep the speed at max!

95 HOLE IN THE WALL

CREATED BY: **ERICTHEPIANOGUY** YEAR: **2009**

A different type of adventure obstacle game, Hole in the Wall was created back in the noughties – but it's a classic and action-packed! The task is to stand in line, then fit through the various holes in a wall that will move towards you. Funny, thrilling and very addictive!

You'll jump through some holes and shapes, or perhaps have to climb a ladder to clear a task. Rounds can be in single or team mode, with the red, blue and yellow team looking to impress. Work out if you need to stand, lie, sit or dive as the wall comes forward!

Clearing 25 walls successfully is classed as hard in this game, so don't beat yourself up if you struggle to get through just four or five at first. Talking of numbers, some rounds need you to add up a quick sum so that you can fit through the correct number. Think fast and move fast!

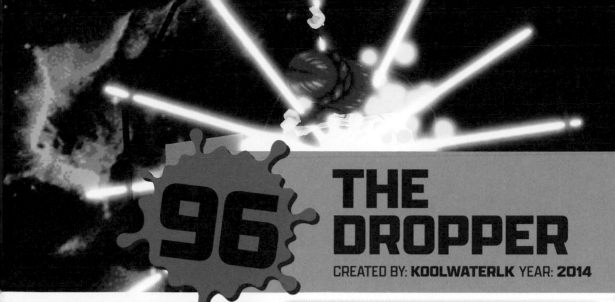

96 THE DROPPER

CREATED BY: **KOOLWATERLK** YEAR: **2014**

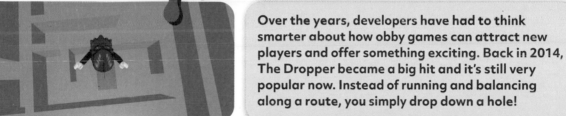

Over the years, developers have had to think smarter about how obby games can attract new players and offer something exciting. Back in 2014, The Dropper became a big hit and it's still very popular now. Instead of running and balancing along a route, you simply drop down a hole!

But, it's not as easy as that of course! When you fall, obstacles and items enter your path and you must move your character to avoid them and complete the stage. Stuff arrives below you quite quickly, so scan ahead and plot the best route to reach the bottom without any contact.

With over 120 themed levels and new maps regularly added, The Dropper keeps things fresh. Falling your way to victory may seem much simpler than more pressure-packed obby platforms, but you need concentration and quick fingers to get in the right spaces to drop like a pro!

97 OBBY BUT YOU CAN'T JUMP

CREATED BY: **SUPER OBBYS :3** YEAR: **2023**

It's a new obby game that the Roblox community loves! The name says it all – it's like a regular obstacle or parkour experience, but you can't jump. So when you reach some of the challenges, work out how to complete them without the ability to jump up into the air!

There's no time limit in this one, so stand back for a few seconds to work out the answer, or perhaps be sneaky and watch another player go through first! Vanishing staircases and objects that won't take your weight are just some of the tricks in this mind-boggling game.

Here's a top tip: if you complete the game, you'll be awarded the famous jump ability and can then show off to the other players! But that feels like cheating, really, because it's much more rewarding to tackle this huge task without being able to jump. Good luck mastering this obby!

JUMP ON IT
Can't wait to complete the game? Enabling jump will cost you 199 Robux!

98 TEAMWORK PUZZLES 2

CREATED BY: **PEAR PRESSURE** YEAR: **2023**

If playing obby games by yourself is not for you, Teamwork Puzzles 2 is the place to be! Here, It's all about working together and following rules as a team. If you don't do that, then levels won't be completed and you won't pick up wins and rewards.

Solutions need to found as part of a duo, trio or four-player team. Stepping on buttons and certain squares will release barriers and ramps, allowing access and progression to the end stage. Don't leave any team member behind and communicate well!

With pets, eggs, VIP passes and special abilities like invisibility and gravity boosts, Teamwork Puzzles 2 has lots of exciting extras and reasons to load it up. Obstacle courses are usually a mad dash to beat every other player, but now you need your friends to get you to the finish!

99 ESCAPE SCHOOL OBBY

CREATED BY: **INTERACTIVE GAMES!** YEAR: **2021**

Sitting in class all day can definitely be a bit boring. So, why not dream of breaking free and escaping from your school? Of course you'd never do that in real-life, but in Roblox it's totally possible. Yay! Load up this awesome obby experience and let your education go wild ...

SHOP WISELY
In the shop, choose from rocket boots, grapple hook, jetpack, speed coil and double jump boosts!

Pull the alarm and run from the class. In the hallways you are faced with lots of obstacle challenges, from jumping over lava to sidestepping slimy stuff and dropping down tunnels. Take each step carefully and remember to trigger each checkpoint so that you spawn in the best place.

There are over 30 stages to clear, including lots of school-based settings. The gym class is tough, followed by a dash through a football field. From stage 18 you'll enter a strange Candy Land dimension, complete with hard new obstacles. Escaping from school isn't easy!

100 ▓▓▓ A▓▓E TH▓ CARNIVAL OF TERROR OBBY!

CREATED BY: **PLATINUMFALLS** YEAR: **2020**

Thousands of Robloxians will be playing this unusual obby at any one time. It's got some comedy scares in places, but you won't be too frightened to remain on mission and try to find your way out of the Carnival of Terror. Complete the challenges and exit to safety!

The evil clown is to blame for you being locked in this strange setting. Hop on the rides and the rollercoasters and always look up, down and all around for clues and ways to beat the traps. There's no time limit, so be cool and calm as you head for each stage's finish.

There's also the chance to teleport to other awesome obby settings and games. Grumpy Gran, Great School Breakout, Barry's Prison Run and Ninja Training Obby will all boost your obstacle and parkour powers. The Carnival is a terror-ific challenge!

YOUNGER FANS' GUIDE

Spending time online is great fun. These games might be your first experience of digital socialising, so here are a few simple rules to help you stay safe and keep the internet an awesome place to spend time:

- **Never give out your real name – don't use it as your username.**
- **Never give out any of your personal details.**
- **Never tell anybody which school you go to or how old you are.**
- **Never tell anybody your password, except a parent or guardian.**
- **Before registering for any account, ask a parent or guardian for permission.**
- **Take regular breaks, as well as playing with parents nearby, or in shared family rooms.**
- **Always tell a parent or guardian if something is worrying you.**

PARENTS' GUIDE

ONLINE CHAT

In most games, there is live on-screen text chat between users. Parents are advised to ensure that their children are only talking to friends and that they aren't being exposed to any adult matter.

SOUND

Sound is crucial in many video games. Players will often wear headphones, meaning parents won't be able to hear what children are listening to. Set up your console or computer to have sound coming from the TV or monitor as well as the headset, so you can hear what your child is experiencing.

REPORTING PLAYERS

If you see or hear a player being abusive, Roblox allows you to report users or interactions. You'll be able to use the Report Abuse links found throughout the site on game pages, but there may also be buttons within chat windows or game menus where you can raise a case with community managers.

SCREEN TIME

Taking regular breaks is important.
Set play sessions by using a timer.
Some games can last a long time and if your child finishes playing in the middle of a round, they could leave their teammates a player short, and lose any points they've earned. It is advisable to give an advanced warning for stopping play or clearly outlining a stopping point before any play session begins.

IN-GAME PURCHASES

Many games offer in-app purchases to enhance the game experience, but they're not required to play the game. They also don't improve a player's performance.
There are ways to set up safety measures on you child's account by setting up a PIN through Settings. Consult these before allowing your child to play any game in order to avoid any unpermitted spending on your account.